NTICS
PROJECTS

We may have different religions, different languages, different colored skin, but we all belong to one human race.

Kofi Annan

© 2020 Publishing Company: NTICS Projects LLC
English title *Refugees, a mission of faith and love*
Original title *Meu maior empreendimento: Uma missão de fé e amor*

Publisher ANDERSON CAVALCANTE
Editors SIMONE PAULINO, LUISA DE MELLO
Editorial assistant JOÃO LUCAS Z. KOSCE
Design ESTÚDIO GRIFO
English version VAUGHN DAVID EASTMAN
Project manager and curator ANA CAROLINA XAVIER
Review and Editorial Assistant PATRICIA MACEDO
Publishing and Adaptation ALINE BISSOLI
Proofreader VANESSA ALMEIDA, MARINA CASTRO
Photo credits CLAUDIO GATTI

Dados Internacionais de Catalogação na Publicação (CIP)
de acordo com ISBD

W835m

Wizard, Carlos
Refugees: a mission of faith and love /
Carlos Wizard
Flórida: NTICS Projects Publishing Company, 2020
144 pp.

ISBN 978-0-578-73903-8

1. Biography. 2. Refugees. 3. Life stories. I. Title.

2020-591   CDD 920
                                        CDD 929

Elaborado por Vagner Rodolfo da Silva, CRB 8/9410
Índices para catálogo sistemático:
1. Biografia 920
2. Biografia 929

CARLOS WIZARD MARTINS

REFUGEES

A MISSION OF FAITH AND LOVE

**All I have left is my one-year-
-old daughter. If I give my
daughter up for adoption,
I will have nothing left.**

*Eduardo Villanueva,
a Venezuelan Refugee*

This book is dedicated to every person whose heart is devoted to bless the soul of a refugee.

I wish I could escape my mind, that I could be free of this world and everything I have seen in the last few years.

Christy Lefteri,
The Beekeeper of Aleppo

We came here to find refuge.
They called us refugees.
So we hid ourselves in their
language until we sounded
just like them. Changed the
way we dressed to look just
like them. Made this our home
until we lived just like them.

J.J. BOLA,
No Place to Call Home

INTRODUCTION

This book narrates facts, challenges, achievements and emotions that I experienced during the 20 months that I spent on the border between Brazil and Venezuela, in the extreme north of the Amazon. It also describes my vision of the humanitarian mission which I voluntarily undertook with the aim of rescuing refugees.

I found out that down deep within each refugee there rages a continuous silent psychological battle, a battle full of dilemmas, insecurity, trauma and uncertainty.

As people flee their country, they flee hunger, misery and misfortune. In spite of fear, they summon the courage to seek a better future trying to save their own life and their family. These people are endowed with tireless resilience as they strive for survival.

On one hand, I've spent almost 2 years on the border north of the Amazon forest, away from the comforts of my home. On the other hand, those refugees left their home country, leaving behind their homes, their professions, their careers, relationships, expectations and dreams.

The most adverse circumstance in life is for one to abandon one's roots, one's culture and one's family, to escape to the unknown, to try to find oneself again.

To flee in search of life, to seek aid, to attempt to find at least a thread of hope, a faint light that may serve as a beacon in the quest for survival is surely one of the most challenging journeys a person can undertake.

No one wants to be a refugee. No one has ever planned to be a refugee. This is something thrust upon the life of thousands of people who, day after day, lose the hope of living in their homeland because of conditions imposed on them against their will. This is the epitome of vulnerability for a human being, who, in spite of a wounded heart, still clings to the hope of finding a sympathetic heart along the way, so that he or she might again believe in life and in some meaning in the face of so much suffering.

And, if there is one thing that nourishes my soul, as I observe the painful path these people follow to escape their present plight, it is their hope. The human hope of being able to begin again and to forge ahead in the face of utmost suffering is something that will never be lost, and that will forever inspire those who see it.

And this book is, above all, about hope, about the love that can be found in the heart of so many people who come together to change the destiny of others. It is about the love that moves people, that moves mountains, that is capable of performing miracles in the day-to-day that is virtually ignored in the headlines of the media.

This book is written in tears, with love, in the emotions that I am unable to restrain within my soul. It is a call for help. It is a sounding alarm so that we will not remain indifferent in the face of a starving refugee. Jesus Christ was the greatest of all refugees. His parents were forced to leave their land and flee to Egypt to escape Herod's sword, who declared death to all male children born at that time. Perhaps this is why Jesus Christ spoke these words:

"For I was an hungered, and ye gave me meat: I was thirsty, and ye gave me drink: I was a stranger, and ye took me in:

Naked, and ye clothed me: I was sick, and ye visited me: I was in prison, and ye came unto me.

Then shall the righteous answer him, saying, Lord, when saw we thee an hungered, and fed thee? or thirsty, and gave thee drink?

When saw we thee a stranger, and took thee in? or naked, and clothed thee?

Or when saw we thee sick, or in prison, and came unto thee?

And the King shall answer and say unto them, Verily I say unto you, Inasmuch as ye have done it unto one of the least of these my brethren, ye have done it unto me." (Matthew 25:35-40)

**Nobody ever wished to be
a refugee.**

Vânia Martins

1

WHY GO TO THE AMAZON BORDER?

I grew up in the outskirts of Curitiba, Brazil, at a time when houses were made of wood and we could easily count our neighbors. Now, here I was at the Campinas airport, with my wife, Vânia, waiting to embark on a new journey. This would be the first time that we would be going to the city of Boa Vista, a small town in the poorest state in Brazil. Vânia looked at me apprehensively. I could see the questions on her face.

"Will we be able to succeed on this mission? What awaits us on the border between Brazil and Venezuela? How can we ever help those refugees?".

And, honestly, I had the same questions. After all, we were leaving the comfort of our home, six children and eighteen grandchildren to go to a far-away place. For the next 2 years, we would be living in a strange land with the charge to help people we didn't even know.

At that moment, I recalled an episode that took place soon after my birth. My mother had married when she was 17 years old. Nine months later, I came into the world. She tells me that soon after I was born, she suddenly felt an immense fear. She had the premonition that she was going to lose her newborn son. Although there was no real reason for her to worry, she was unable to rid herself of that feeling.

One night, she opened the Bible and read a few verses that made her feel comforted. She then asked God, with a feeling that only a mother can muster as she prayed:

"Save this child's life, Lord! Do not let anything bad happen to him. I promise to raise him so that he will serve Thee. May this child grow to serve God. I will do everything to guide and prepare him in Thy way."

To this very day, I still remember hearing this story many times during my childhood and adolescence. This experience has always influenced me, especially when I faced moments of decision.

And this was one of those moments. We were at the airport in Campinas, about to depart for a humanitarian and altruistic labor dedicated to our fellow beings. But that was not the first time we had left on a mission. 18-year-old youth, members of the Church of Jesus Christ of Latter-day Saints have their first experience as volunteers when they embark on a two-year mission. Their assignment may be to any of more than 400 locations around the world. It is a challenge for which they are prepared from the time they are children. By serving their fellow beings, they mature and become self-sufficient adults. They serve a total of 730 days on a mission that might completely change only one life, perhaps their own, and consequently may alter the destiny of many others.

That is the experience that I had when I was 19 years old, when I said good-bye to my family in Curitiba and left for Portugal. After 2 years, I returned home a different person. At the same time, Vânia had accepted the call to spend 18 months in Rio de Janeiro, doing the same voluntary work.

Although I had been in love with her since I was 15 years old, she had never given me the time of day. She would say that I was very childish and light-hearted, never taking anything serious. After my return from that mission, she seemed to see another man in me. Once she saw me with other eyes, we began a story together which would bring us experiences we could have never imagined.

After we had been married for 20 years, one day Elder Jeffery R. Holland, an apostle of the Church, came to visit our home during a visit to Brazil. In a personal interview, he surprised us when he said: "God has an important calling for you both. For the next 3 years, you will preside over a mission of the Church. We will let you know where later".

We immediately thanked him for the confidence and accepted the call, knowing that it was a divine calling. In order for you to understand the context, each mission consists of about 200 young people between 18 and 20 years old and is supervised by a couple who voluntarily serve for 3 years, being responsible for the care, well-being and guidance of the missionaries.

Those 3 years we spent on the northeastern part of Brazil represented a hat in all our personal, professional and business interests. We were conscious of the divine nature of that call, which gave us comfort instead of any distress. Nevertheless, we met great challenges, obstacles and necessary adaptations. However, we had the conviction that that time did not belong to us. It was a sacred time.

It was a time in which we needed to dedicate our efforts, talents, abilities and gifts to the service of our fellow beings. That was 24 hours a day, seven days a week, without holidays, interruptions or absences, and without trips away from the mission territory. We were there to serve. We were accompanied by our daughters, Thais and Priscila, who were, by then 14 and 12 years old, and Nicholas and Felipe who were 3 and 1 year old. Our twin sons, Charles and Lincoln, 19 years of age, were away from Brazil serving their own missions, too. The entire family was engaged in a single purpose, and this fact also greatly strengthened us. In spite of the distance, it united us.

At the time we were to serve our humanitarian mission, I was over 60 years old, owner of several successful companies, with plenty of money and time; Vânia and I could have gone anywhere in the world: Hawaii, Alaska, Asia, Western Europe, the Mediterranean, you name it. However, we felt it was time to offer humanitarian service and this was supposed to be different from the other missions we had experienced up to this point. We were heading toward a place where we would be receiving and sheltering Venezuelan refugees fleeing across the border and arriving in Brazil in search of dignity and better living conditions.

Since I made the decision to serve, every week people would ask me:

"Carlos, what makes you leave the comfort of your home in Campinas, your businesses, your mansion in Orlando, your Ferrari in the garage and go to the Amazon to aid Venezuelans?"

It was an elegant and polite way of asking "What has gotten into you? Have you gone crazy? Have you turned into a monk and made a vow of poverty?"

Whenever I encounter that question, I give a romantic answer. I calmly explain that when I got married, I was earning minimum wage. We left for our honeymoon in a borrowed old vw van and on a certain evening, sitting beside a beautiful beach in Brazil, we discussed our goals for the future. One of the goals had been to seek prosperity! I believe that God heard and fulfilled our heart's desire. Later on, I went to study at the Brigham Young University in Utah. I then returned to Brazil and began to teach English lessons in my home. I started with one student, then two, then three. After some time, following my entrepreneurial spirit, I decided to open an English school, which, given enough time, became the largest language teaching system in the world. In total, Wizard had 3,000 schools, offering 50,000 jobs in several different countries around the world and serving a million students per year. Later, I sold my company to Pearson for 750 million dollars. I am sure God was generous to us, He granted us with the desire of our heart and blessed us with much more than we ever could have possibly ever imagined.

I then explain that a person generally has four stages in life. From birth to 20 years of age is the stage of acquiring education, the acquisition of knowledge. From 20 to 30 years of age is the definition stage, that is, when the people choose the path they will follow to fulfill themselves personally and professionally. From 30 to 60 years of age is the achievement stage. That is, people will seek to fulfil their dreams in all aspects. After 60 years of age, is the time to enjoy what has been accomplished and to dedicate part of their time, resources and abilities contributing to the well-being of society.

Upon hearing the explanation above, people get all emotional, they congratulate me, they applaud, and I am pleased with having given a satisfactory answer to an enigmatic and recurring question. But today, I am going to tell you the truth. That was not the real reason I made the radical decision to move to Boa Vista to assume that humanitarian mission. The real reason is printed on the cover of this book. However, for you to fully understand my motivation, you need to be aware of two important episodes, which I will narrate in the next two chapters.

It is the obligation of every person born in a safer room to open the door when someone in danger knocks.

Dina Nayeri, Refuge, a Novel

2

BETWEEN LIFE AND DEATH

One evening, when my twin sons, Charles and Lincoln were 18 years old, one evening, I was in a meeting at the company when my secretary interrupted me saying:

"Mr. Martins, there is an urgent phone call for you." *Who could be calling me at this time of the day? It was already 6:30 p.m.,* I wondered. I hurried to take the call, not knowing what to expect and this is what I heard on the other end of the line:

"Carlos, this is Izabel, Vania's friend. Come quickly. Your sons have suffered an automobile accident. Come immediately. The situation is critical."

As I approached the accident, traffic was heavy. My apprehension only got worse. The police directed traffic to other streets and everything was in chaos. I will never forget the horns blaring, the traffic jams, the sound of sirens, and the nervous drivers all around. And I was the most nervous of them all. The officers were blocking access to the scene of the accident, but I kept insisting. I needed to get past the barriers because the boys in the car were my sons. Finally, they allowed me to pass.

The scene seemed even more critical and alarming than Izabel had described: police officers, firefighters, paramedics, ambulances, rubberneckers, and news people were everywhere.

Everything that I would see from that point on would be engraved forever in my memory. In the middle of the road sat a heavy tractor, which had collided head-on with the car in which my twin sons were riding. Full of fear, I approached the car and they told me that my son Lincoln had been driving, but the driver's seat was empty. I didn't see him anywhere. In the passenger's seat I thought I saw my son Charles unconscious, pinned in by the twisted wreckage. Was he alive? How could I know? In the confusion, I tried to keep my composure and my heart beat heavily in my ears.

A police officer approached me.

"Are you the twins' father?"

"Yes," I answered, still shocked by the scene.

His answer was the kind of sentence no father should hear in his life, especially in the way it was delivered.

"I'm sorry. You have just lost one son. We are trying to save the other."

That is when the ground came out from under me. It was as if a pit had opened below my feet. This was the most tragic news that a father could receive. Out of nowhere, Izabel appeared, trying to comfort me. I immediately told her:

"I need you to go to our house and prepare Vânia for this. She is not ready to receive such news."

I then rushed to the hospital where they had taken my son. When I arrived there, they informed me that there had been a third person in the back seat of the car. That information also caught me off guard. Who could have been the third passenger?

Soon thereafter, I was told that it was a friend of my sons and in that moment, totally bewildered, I saw an ambulance pull in and a body was removed from it. Someone made the comment:

"This one's gone."

Certain that I had lost one son, I phoned three friends to tell them of the tragedy.

Vânia suddenly arrived. She was weeping openly, we embraced. In that embrace, I perceived that she had no precise information as to the nature of the accident. She only knew that our sons were being attended to.

That is when a nurse came to us and announced:

"We are trying to save Charles. He is undergoing surgery at this very moment."

I was confused. I had been told that I had lost my son. I thought that I had seen my son in the wreckage of the car in the passenger's seat. I pulled the nurse to the side and asked:

"Are you saying this to calm my wife down? You are afraid to tell her the truth, aren't you?"

"That is the truth!" she said. "We are trying to save the boy. He suffered head trauma, internal hemorrhage, a compound fracture to one leg, his spleen was perforated and he broke his arm in seven places. He is unconscious in the ICU between life and death..."

"Please, don't try to fool me," I insisted.

"That is the truth. You can believe me. Your son is alive."

Those words inspired a flame of hope and faith in me. *Maybe Charles really was still alive. That is, maybe he still had a chance of surviving,* I thought. However, I couldn't hold it back and I asked:

"Well then, who died?"

"The other passenger in the car. The one who was in the front passenger's seat. He is the one who died."

"So, where was Charles?" I asked, breathing deeply.

"He was in the back seat. Upon the impact of the accident, he was thrown out of the car."

When I arrived at the accident scene, I was given such a shock that I could have sworn that I had seen my son pinned in the wreckage, sitting in the front passenger's seat. Could it have been my despair, a hallucination? That image will never leave my mind.

I am simply unable to exactly describe the sensation of learning that my son was alive, even if he was between life and death.

Later that night, the doctors finally made a more detailed evaluation of the boys' medical condition. Lincoln, who had been in the driver's seat, was well. Charles was in very serious condition, but had a chance of survival. The doctors advised us: "Go home. It is late. You need to rest. There is nothing you can do here at the hospital."

That verdict kept echoing around in my thoughts. There was really not much for us to do at the hospital. We went home and Vânia kept repeating:

"What does God want to show us with this accident?" What does the Lord want me to do for Him to save my son's life? For some reason, that night, as we were unable to fall asleep, one thought kept coming to Vania's mind: *I have four brothers who, in addition to their biological children, adopted other children.* Vânia had always told her brothers: "I already have four children. I don't want any more. It's too much responsibility and work. Too much dedication is required to raise a child."

She would say that she admired her brothers' initiative, but that she would not adopt any children. That had always been her line.

"I just don't have the energy and patience for that. Adopting a child requires total commitment."

But, after fitfully tossing and turning that night, the next morning, Vânia had a very strong feeling. It was an inspiration in the form of a prayer:

"Dear God, I ask Thee with all my heart to save my son's life. If my prayer is answered, I promise that I will care for one of Thy children who has been abandoned in this world."

I was kneeling beside her and was very surprised with that reaction. For the first time in Vania's life, she considered the possibility of adopting a less fortunate child. After she prayed and shared with me that feeling, I immediately supported her. I then said to her:

"Sweetheart, if you are prepared to adopt a child, I have that same desire. So, let's adopt two children. You care for one and I will care for the other."

As incredible as it may seem, that comment made her smile and we both smiled in the midst of that utterly turbulent moment. It was as though that desire had already been part of our heart for a long time. As though we had been born with that feeling inside us. We knew that adopting two children was what God expected us to do.

After 11 days in a coma in the ICU, Charles had his first reaction: His eyes blinked. The next day, there was a slight movement in his fingers. In spite of his inability to move, after a few days, he was released from the hospital because of the possibility of contracting hospital infection.

Charles came home conscious, but unable to move. Of the 155 lbs. he had weighed at the time of the accident, he now weighed less than 130 lbs. He was like an 18-year-old baby. He could not eat, go to the bathroom, walk or bathe by himself. He could leave home only in a wheelchair.

With the help of a team of physical and speech therapists and psychologists, after months of treatment, he was able to walk again. At the end of six months, there was another dramatic moment. He and his brother were to be separated for the first time.

The twins had prepared themselves from childhood to go on missions. Lincoln was approved, but not Charles. He still needed some corrective surgery on his arm and on his hand. The twins talked about it and decided that Lincoln wouldn't need to wait. He could go ahead on the mission that awaited him.

A young man does not choose where he is to serve. This mission call comes from the president of the Church in Salt Lake City. After the Church receives and analyzes all of the papers, a destiny is determined. There is no obligation for any youth to serve a mission, that is, it is a personal and voluntary decision. But if the individual feels this divine calling within his heart, he leaves to serve that mission.

The mission is most certainly an enriching and sacred experience. I like to think of Jesus' words when he said "For whosoever will save his life shall lose it: and whosoever will lose his life for my sake shall find it." So, the young person who enters the mission and the adult who comes out of it are different persons.

The mission, because of its spiritual nature, gives a new dimension to the purpose of one's very existence. These young people become aware that they are legitimate children of a loving God. They are then able to approach this divine source and feel the presence of that intimate relationship with the Creator in their thoughts and intuitions. This brings them peace, serenity and confidence to overcome challenges. In addition to this, it fills them with the ability to dream and go after those dreams, knowing that God will be at their side, giving them His support, inspiration and protection on the road to their infinite potential.

It was with that feeling that Lincoln opened the envelope, which contained his life's destiny for the next 2 years. He was called to Houston, Texas.

The twins shared a hug at the airport. Lincoln left, knowing that his brother would soon fulfill his childhood dream. Charles stayed behind, knowing that he would soon follow in his brother's footsteps.

Six months later, Charles was approved to serve a mission. At that moment in time, although I knew this was his most ardent desire, my heart was anxious. Deep inside, both Vânia and I thought he might be assigned somewhere close to Campinas. In case some medical care would become necessary, we would be able to come quickly to his aid. When he finally opened the envelope containing his call, he found out that he would spend the next 2 years in Mozambique.

And so, Charles embarked for Africa, with the conviction that he was doing the will of God.

3

"NICHOLAS, CATCH THE BALL!"

With Lincoln in Texas and Charles in Africa, Vânia and I did not forget our commitment to God. We went to the Adoption Agency and filled out the paperwork for adoption. Our intent was to adopt two boys. What was the waiting period? One or 2 years. That would be the "pregnancy" period for our little boys.

After more than a year, one day I received a call from a small town back in the interior of Brazil.

"Mr. Martins, you are registered to adopt a child, is that not so?" said a voice on the other end of the line.

"Yes! Yes! Yes! That's us", I answered. I was anxious to hear what they had to say.

"Well, we have a three-month-old boy and we are looking for a family for him. Your papers have been approved. Could you come to get him? If you are willing, the child is yours."

"Yes! Yes! Yes! We will come this very day!" was my response.

It was difficult to repress the emotion of that moment. I told Vânia, we gathered a change of clothes, we got the girls ready, Thais and Priscila, who were overjoyed with the news and we rushed out to meet our new son.

We were very well received at the Adoption Agency where they explained all the necessary formalities. During the conversation, we asked:

"By any chance, would there be another child in this town who is ready to be adopted? In our application, we had offered to adopt two boys." The judge looked at the city social worker and asked:

"Doesn't this boy have a two-year-old brother?"

The answer came quickly.

"Yes, Your Honor, he has. But the paperwork for his adoption is not complete." Then the Judge told us:

"If you would like, we can try to prepare the paperwork. If all goes well, instead of one, you can take the two little brothers."

Even today, I get emotional when I recall that moment. We feel that the unseen hand of God was there, preparing each step of the way. How could we have known that in that little town there were two little brothers waiting for their adoptive parents to appear?

And that is how the recently-born baby got the name of Felipe. The 2 years old was Nicholas. When we got back to Campinas, the two girls wanted to play with Nicholas.

Their first thought was "boys like to play ball" and so they went and got a ball.

"Come on, Nicholas, catch the ball." they would say.

The boy simply stood there as if he had not heard them. "Nicholas, come play with us". No reaction. Nothing. His eyes were fixed on nothing.

Vânia, who was watching that interaction, had the strange sensation that he didn't know what the words "ball" or "play" meant. At other times, he would sit on the sofa, watching television, without making a single gesture, without making any sound, he wouldn't ask for anything and he never smiled. There was never any interaction or communication. We soon perceived that something was not right. Was the boy deaf, mute, or who knows, perhaps autistic? Besides, he had no motor skills, not even to hold a pencil.

After a series of evaluations, specialists supposed that during birth, the boy may have suffered a lack of oxygen to the brain, which caused some long-term effects.

In addition, they surmised that during his first 2 years, Nicholas must have been isolated, without interactions with other children or adults, so that because of a lack of stimuli, his cognitive development had been seriously compromised. When he began to attend school, teachers and coordinators noticed that his learning, assimilation and apprehension skills were somewhat lacking. Even when playing video games, he would call Felipe, who was 2 years younger than him, to help him pass from one level to another.

Later on, Nicholas was diagnosed with a certain degree of autism or Asperger's syndrome. With this diagnosis, Nicholas became a special-needs student who required special teachers. However, schools in general did not understand and could not attend to his needs. They often refused to give him any special attention. As a result, from one year to the next, he would be transferred between different schools. In all, he attended six different schools. His brother, Felipe, who had no learning difficulty at all, to show solidarity with his brother, went with him whenever he changed schools. Only through the aid of dozens of hired private tutors, did Nicholas succeed in graduating from high school at age 20.

None of this was a challenge for us. It was all part of our mission, the commitment we had made, as parents, to be, for him, the safe haven where he could be guided through a life in which he could develop his capacities.

After his graduation from high school, he would encounter a great challenge. From the time that they were little children, both Nicholas and Felipe had said that when they grew to be old enough, they would both go to serve a mission. To be approved for missionary service, each youth submits to a series of exams to evaluate his physical and emotional condition. Felipe passed in all of the interviews and medical exams and was approved for missionary service. He received his call, and was assigned to serve two years in the Irvine, California mission.

So, what about Nicholas? There was never any doubt in his mind that he would be a missionary like his parents, older brothers, his friends at Church and even like his younger brother Felipe, who already had his call in his hands. Nevertheless, Vânia had her doubts and worries. She would lose sleep and became apprehensive whenever she thought about it.

What if he was not approved?

How would he react?

Would he understand?

How would he feel?

Would he become depressed?

Would he overcome it?

Would he feel even more marginalized?

What about his friends? What would they say?

Would they discriminate even more against him?

At the same time, she even wondered about her son's capabilities.

Would he have the necessary abilities?

Would he have enough maturity to deal with mission rules and demands?

Would he get along well with his companions?

Was he ready to make decisions and be a self-sufficient young man?

Would it be a positive and satisfying experience for him?

All these dilemmas remained in Vania's mind. She was the one who had wished the adoption of this boy, with the intention of helping him to overcome all his challenges. We knew that this was our mission, as parents, to support him in reaching his full potential without encouraging unrealistic expectations in him.

For whatever reason, while Vânia worried, I maintained a certain degree of confidence, of faith and optimism that everything would turn out right. The day finally arrived when Nicholas was to see a doctor who would evaluate his condition. Vânia and I waited outside the office, rooting for everything to turn out positively. The emotions were somewhat like those of an expectant father, at the maternity center awaiting the arrival of a newborn child.

Out of that office would come the answer concerning the destiny of our son. Either he would be approved and forge ahead in fulfilling his dream, or he might encounter frustration in having failed in his hopes to do the voluntary work that he so desired.

After almost an hour of waiting, Nicholas and the doctor came out of the office. Vânia and I were anxious to hear some comment, some word, some definition. All we wanted to hear at that moment was a YES from the doctor. However, he made no comment. He said nothing. He gave no sign of hope. He only said: "You will receive the results in two weeks." Vânia wept inside with anguish. Not wanting to show her feelings to the boy, she comforted him, saying that God's will would prevail. In our hearts, however, both she and I foresaw the results. We were already considering how we would deal with the situation. How we would explain the results to Nicholas. Finally, when we received the negative decision, we did not have the courage to immediately tell him because he was anxious, expecting to leave for "his mission" at any moment.

Over the years, in decisive moments of our life together, Vania's inspiration, attitude and strength have always had a great impact on our destiny. Upon concluding my first semester at BYU, when I got poor grades and decided to abandon everything and return to Brazil, I went home to our basement apartment and told her about my intention.

At that very moment, I found out who I had married. Vânia firmly stated: "You have come to America to get an education. You cannot give up in your first semester. What will our children say of their father. Put something in your mind Carlos, we will only return to Brazil after you have graduated." At that moment I knew I had no escape. After my graduation, while I was working for a company in Hamilton, Ohio, a friend from India convinced me that I should stay in the United States and apply for citizenship. When I presented this idea to Vânia, she was again adamant: "Absolutely not! We will return to Brazil and we will seek prosperity in Brazil. You will find the American dream in our own country."

But now, how would we break that news to Nicholas? One morning, Vânia awoke with a radiant look on her face, as though she had had a marvelous dream. It was an impression that had come to her that morning.

"Carlos, now I know what we are going to do. I already have the answer. I know how we can deal with Nicholas' issue.

I was both surprised and curious."

"So, just tell me, at once! Now I'm the one who is nervous and anxious, unsure of how to tell our son."

She seemed to have the right answer right on the tip of her tongue.

"My goodness! Why didn't we think of this before? You are certainly aware of the senior couple missionary program in the Church. So, why can't we offer to serve a mission together?"

"Yes, but what about Nicholas?" I asked.

"He can go with us." she said. "He will accompany us. All three of us will go together, to the same place."

"Do you suppose the Church will accept this arrangement?" was my question.

"And why not? We will be with him the entire time. Who can better take care of a son than his parents?"

"That's right. That makes sense. But, wait a minute. You are suggesting that you and I leave the family, children, grandchildren, home, companies, our business, and go off to some unknown place without knowing where we will be and what we will be doing?"

"Exactly. After all, God has given us everything we ever imagined and much more. What will a father and mother do to meet the needs of a child? He is young. He has everything ahead of him. This would be the fulfillment of a dream for him. Let's not rob him of this opportunity.

I told Vânia that I would discuss this with Lincoln, one of our twins. I wanted to hear what he thought of this plan. He supported the idea out of hand, but said that it would be best to find out more about this possibility from Church leaders.

"To be honest, dad, I have never heard of a similar situation before, but if you allow it, I will make some inquiries to verify this possibility." I thanked him for his support and gave him total liberty to make the inquiries.

The Church of Jesus Christ of Latter-day Saints has a Brazil Area Presidency, located in São Paulo. When Lincoln called the president of the church in Brazil, the conversation went something like this:

"Lincoln, do you believe in miracles?" the president asked on the other end of the line.

"Of course, I do, but why do you ask?"

"Do you believe that God directs His work?" he continued.

"I fully believe it." Lincoln answered.

"Well, then, I am going to tell you something. Only a half hour ago, we finished a meeting. We had the impression that we needed to call a couple to serve a humanitarian mission on the Brazil - Venezuela border for the purpose of assisting refugees. We had no couple in mind. We can only imagine that your call was the answer to our prayers."

As soon as we heard that story, our hearts filled with emotion, gratitude and joy. In an incomprehensible way, we knew that God was once more guiding our steps. It was a miracle.

That same week, Vânia and I were interviewed in São Paulo by Elder Marcus Aidukaitis, who was at that time the highest authority of the Church in Brazil.

"So, do you accept this call?" he asked, already knowing our answer.

"Yes. We would like to serve as volunteers for the period of 1 year."

Then, something came that we weren't expecting.

"But, we need you for 2 years, not just one. What do you say to that?"

That news left no doubt in our minds that this mission would be a challenge. It would not be just for our convenience, but to comply with a divine plan.

"If this is what the Lord desires, we are ready to serve."

"I am sure that this will be an unforgettable experience for you both and for your son, Nicholas" The president promised.

"When do we start?" I asked.

"As soon as possible, because the situation in Venezuela is very critical" He concluded.

We knew that we were to spend the months of April and May in Canada, since Nicholas was going to take a cognitive development course in Toronto. We are Brazilians. We love soccer. Throughout June and July we will go to Moscow with our children and grandchildren to watch the World Cup.

"Can we begin in August?" I asked.

"O.K. agreed. You will begin in August."

He then explained that the Church has a special interest in caring for refugees in several places in the world, including Syria, North Africa, Haiti and now it was our time to take care of refugees from Venezuela. These are people who have found themselves in a state of extreme vulnerability. Without food, without water, without work, without schools for their children, without medical attention, without minimal conditions of dignity in their lives.

When we explained all this to Nicholas, he understood, accepted and became excited about heading for the Amazon in this humanitarian mission. On August 3, 2018, Vânia, Nicholas and I left for the little town of Boa Vista in the north of Brazil, certain that we were doing the right thing. In our hearts we had one conviction. We were answering a divine call. This was the plan that God had prepared for us to follow at this time in our lives.

In the months previous to our departure, often, as I prepared myself mentally for this new mission, as I meditated on everything that was happening, in the still of the night, I would wonder:

What would have happened if Nicholas had caught the ball?
What if he had readily played with his sisters?
What if he had passed the medical evaluation?

In those moments of reflection, a verse from the Bible would come to mind:

"**For my thoughts are not your thoughts, neither are your ways my ways, saith the Lord. For as the heavens are higher than the earth, so are my ways higher than your ways, and my thoughts than your thoughts.**" (Isaiah 55:8-9)

The world will not be destroyed by those who do evil, but by those who watch them without doing anything.

Albert Einstein

4

WELCOME TO THE AMAZON

"Ladies and Gentlemen, this is the captain speaking. We are approaching our destination, and in a few moments we will be landing in Boa Vista. Return your seat backs in their upright position, close the trays in front of you and fasten your seatbelts. Crew, prepare for landing. The local temperature is 105 degrees."

We gathered our luggage and when we exited the arrival area, to our surprise, we were met by president Caetano and his wife, Sister Caetano, the couple who supervised the work of 200 young missionaries in the Amazon region.

"What a coincidence to find you here at the airport!" We said.

"Not a coincidence! My wife and I traveled 500 miles and are here to welcome you." He then greeted our son:

"So, you must be Nicholas. Here is your missionary name tag. We already have a companion waiting for you."

I was surprised and apprehensive about this immediate response from the mission president. Was it possible that he was unaware of Nicholas' special condition?

Later on, he explained that he had been impressed by our decision to leave on a mission in order to give this unique experience to our son. In light of that fact, he said: "Since mother and father are in town, we can try to leave Nicholas with a companion for a couple of weeks, maybe a month. If something unexpected happens he will immediately return home and the three of you will proceed in your mission as originally planned. Let's see how he comes out. If he is ok for one month, maybe he can try a second month under normal missionary conditions, following mission standards, rules and daily routines. We will leave Nicholas in God's hands".

Surprised and at the same time overjoyed, Vânia and I accepted, supported and thanked President Caetano for this unexpected show of support for our son. Nicholas would seek our help only in the event of an emotional, personal or interpersonal nature, or some emergency or out-of-control situation. From that moment on, every day we prayed that God would give him give him wisdom, intelligence, protection, and positive experiences, both for him and for his brother, Felipe, in California.

This was our first time in Boa Vista. We went to live in the only residential building in the city. We left an eleven thousand square foot home to live in a tiny apartment. Here, I need to make an observation. One of my wife's greatest frustrations after marrying me was to discover that her husband didn't have a single home maintenance skill. Vânia has always loved remodeling, upgrades and construction. All these things are very normal, even therapeutic to her. For me, they are torture. I had never even hung a picture on a wall. That is how we came to know Geraldo in Boa Vista.

Vânia needed to set up a washer and dryer, air conditioning, chandeliers, Internet and basic home services. A friend from the Church referred us to Geraldo, who quickly solved all of these problems.

I soon asked him:

"Geraldo, what is your profession? Where do you work?"

With a broad smile and joyful look, he answered without blinking:

"I work for myself, doing odd jobs as they are needed."

"I am going to live here on the border for 2 years. Would you like to be my assistant?" I asked.

Geraldo is a calm kind of a guy in the way he talks and expresses himself. He simply asked:

"Doing what?"

The truth is, I didn't quite know the answer. But it was clear that I would need someone with his profile at my side; A person with a good heart and up for any challenge.

"Well, I'm not quite sure. I just arrived in town. But it will be a humanitarian mission. We will be receiving and assisting Venezuelans who arrive in Brazil."

"Oh, I get it. You will be opening a company in town to offer work to those people." He commented.

"No, Geraldo, I did not come here to do business. This will be humanitarian work. I don't know yet just what I will be doing, but we can find that out together."

"I've heard people talk about you. I don't know what you're planning, but count me in. When do I start?" he asked.

"You have already started. Welcome to the humanitarian mission."

With a handshake, we began our partnership.

Geraldo was born in the Amazon region and when the Venezuelan crisis erupted, he moved to Boa Vista. I am always impressed when I see that wherever the greatest need arises, there you can find the biggest hearts. Hearts that love others, although they be strangers, who are willing to help those in need, and who do for others in a single day more than some do in a lifetime.

In the very first week at Boa Vista, Vânia invited me to go shopping for some homemaking items. Someone suggested that we go to a specialized store. As we were leaving the store, going to the cash register to pay for our purchases, I was interrupted.

"Excuse me, but are you Mr. Carlos Wizard?"

"Yes, that's my name, what is yours?"

"I am Rafael Rocha, I own the Pizza Hut franchise in the city of Manaus ."

"Oh, that is great. So then, we are business partners."

"What brings you to this little town? Are you here to make some investment? Are you surveying the market?" he asked.

"No, no, nothing like that." I responded, without giving many details.

"Well, perhaps you are here to buy up some land, to take advantage of the great land prices here." He was curious.

"Not that, either. I am here with my wife on a humanitarian mission. I might be able to explain it better to you later."

Being very cordial, courteous and kind, Rafael invited us to lunch together and to meet his wife, Adilane. In this way, a friendship was born, which lasted throughout the 20 months that we lived in that town.

As we became better acquainted, he admitted that the day he first saw me in the store, he never imagined that I would be there on a humanitarian mission. They were amazed to learn that it would be possible to do charity, when I was a businessman with so many successful companies. The impression that they had of me was of a rational man who did not consider his fellow man or the spiritual side of life and, little by little, they admitted that they, too, were changing their attitude in life. They had been focusing a lot on work and had neglected the spiritual aspect of life. As we became closer, they perceived that our inner strength stemmed from our faith and that fueling that strength was a matter of choice. One day Adilane said: "I feel everyone is able to choose to set aside moments for God and consider what we can do for our fellow beings".

So, they began to attend Church meetings with us on Sundays and realized how their lives became lighter, more well balanced. Rafael told me once that his load of work was still heavy, but that he felt stronger to direct his personal and professional decisions, more calmly and with greater clarity, and that he had more discernment to set his priorities.

As for Adilane, she got in touch with friends who made medical supply donations and helped us in the humanitarian cause of aiding the refugees. In this way, she began getting involved and participating in serving others.

When they felt that they were more and more in tune with God, they made a decision. After having been together for 19 years, they decided to officially get married. On August 9, 2019, they were married and the next day they asked to be baptized into the Church of Jesus Christ of Latter-day Saints.

I was clear from the start that it was very difficult to find anyone who had been born in Boa Vista. To tell the truth, I believe that the ratio is about one Boa Vista native in every 10 people. The people there come from all over Brazil.

Another observation is that in Boa Vista, there are very few work opportunities. Most of the employed work for the government. In that small town is located every federal, state and of course, Municipal agency is located. The remainder are employed in local commerce or receive aid from federal government programs. There is no industry or large companies. Besides that, 50% of the lands in the state of Roraima, of which Boa Vista is the capital, is designed as Indians reservations.

For you to have an idea of the Indians' influence in the state, on the highway that connects Boa Vista to the city of Manaus, a distance of 500 miles, there is a stretch of about 125 miles within the indigenous reserve on which traffic is allowed only from 6 a.m. to 6 p.m. During the other 12 hours, the highway is closed by the Indians, with the authorization of the federal government. As I have been told, this is so that the Indians' sleep will not be disturbed.

We had our home set up, shopping done, and everything was in order for us to begin the work we had come to do. One night, before we went to bed, Vânia asked me:

"Carlos, exactly what day did we arrive in Boa Vista?"

I grabbed my cell phone and checked.

"We arrived on August 3, 2018."

Vânia did a double take and choked up with emotion. She recalled:

"What an incredible thing. What a coincidence. It was exactly 20 years ago, on August 3, 1998, that our twin sons suffered that awful automobile accident, which in time resulted in Nicholas coming into our home. And on that very day, he initiated his mission here in Boa Vista, and consequently, we are together on the border between Brazil and Venezuela united in this humanitarian cause."

With deep emotion in face of that incredible coincidence of dates, I was reminded of a thought given by Elder Neal A. Maxwell:

"You and I may call these intersecting moments 'coincidence.' This word is understandable for mortals to use, but *coincidence* is not an appropriate word to describe the workings of an omniscient God. He does not do things by 'coincidence' but ... by 'divine design.'"

5

OPERATION GOODWILL

Imagine now that you have been transported to a remote locale on this planet crowded with refugees. Try to visualize hundreds of people arriving each day. Wearing ragged clothing, some carrying a small valise, others carrying a backpack as their luggage. They arrive without a place to stay, a place to bathe, a place to eat, or a place to sleep at night. They come seeking refuge and shelter, crowding around the bus station and churches. The day gets dark and these refugees arrange themselves at random, some leaning on each other, some sleeping on cardboard, mothers with small children, others nursing their infants in arms. There are children, young people, adults, the elderly. All are exposed to the elements, to the rain that falls during the night or to the stifling heat of the day. Now, imagine that with noon the scalding sun at the equator has sent the thermometer to 105º. A crowd of people surrounds a truck parked by the bus station, distributing boxed lunches to those who have nothing to eat. Visualize hundreds of people pushing and shoving, trying to get close to the truck, fearful that there would not be enough food and that someone in the family would have to go without eating that day. That was the scene we encountered in August of 2018 when we arrived in Boa Vista.

During our first trips to the supermarket, it was common to be standing in line to pay and, as we looked back, we would see a young mother with a child in her arms and a few items in a basket. Upon arriving at the cashier, she would ask:

"Excuse me, sir, would you please pay for this food for me and my child? My baby is hungry."

In such a moment, you look at your own cart full of food, you look back and see the emptiness in that mother's eyes with the single hope that some Good Samaritan will alleviate her pain by paying for a few basic items. And that malnourished child in her arms. How could you deny food in the face of such a circumstance?

One of the first persons I met was a businesswoman by the name of Aurea Cruz, who left her business to feed thousands of people every day at the local Catholic church. Every time I think of her, my heart is filled with appreciation for this incredible woman, her example of selflessness, of love and dedication to the refugees.

During the first days in Boa Vista, I was invited to attend a coordination meeting of the agencies participating in Operation Goodwill. For this meeting conducted by the Brazilian Army, representatives gather from dozens of national and international agencies that give support to refugees.

That was where I met Mr. Kanaan, one of the most human military men I have ever had the pleasure of meeting. It was the first time I had ever worked in conjunction with a military operation. And, lacking any experience, I began by committing a *gaffe* when I addressed Mr. Kanaan, who was the Colonel in charge, the main coordinator of Operation Goodwill, except for General Pazuello who commanded the entire Operation Goodwill.

"So, Lieutenant Kanaan, my name is Carlos, this is my wife Vânia and for the next 2 years we will be by your side to help you in any way we can." He looked at me in a strange way and he must have thought:

Where did this guy come from if he can't even tell the difference in rank between a Lieutenant and a Colonel in the Armed Forces?

A year later, when I held my birthday party in Boa Vista, I was sharing some of the interesting things that we had experienced in the city. I told my guests about how I had called our great Colonel a Lieutenant on the first day I met him. After my little speech, my friend Kanaan, who was at the party, called me aside, and rewound the messages on his cell phone and showed me a recording of my mistake when I called him a Lieutenant a year ago. I imagine he will never forgive me for that *gaffe*.

I later came to admire the spirit and humanity of this great man Colonel Kanaan. I once asked him how he dealt with so many day-to-day emotions while working with Operation Goodwill. He shared the following with me:

"We are engaged in a continuous marathon of aiding people. There is often no time to become emotional. We are involved in the Operation all day, but when I return to my lodging at night, I sometimes fall apart. Then I feel the weight of the responsibility of deciding the destiny of each immigrant. I often wonder if a mother with a child in arms will survive. Will she find a way to provide food for her child the next day?. Sometimes it's hard to hold back the tears."

He told me that on one Christmas Eve, a group of military men filled a truck with food packages. Their plan was to distribute the food to the refugees. When they arrived at the distribution site, a 12-year-old boy rode up to them on an old bicycle and asked them for a food package. At that moment, colonel Kanaan decided to play a joke and made the boy a proposition:

"You have a bicycle. We can make a deal. If you would like, I will trade the food package for your bicycle." Of course, the Colonel said this in a playful way. He just wanted to see the boy's reaction. To his amazement, the boy answered:

"OK, it's a deal. You can keep the bicycle. I will take the food."

The soldiers who were with the Colonel were surprised. They turned and asked:

"Colonel, are you going to keep the poor boy's bicycle? What will we ever do with this child's old bicycle?"

"We made a bargain. You may put the bicycle in the truck." ordered the Colonel.

In the army, no one questions the orders of one's superiors, especially coming from Colonel Kanaan.

The boy said goodbye to his bicycle, grabbed the food package and walked over to his mother and sister. It was obvious that Colonel Kanaan had no intention to keep the bicycle. He then walked over the boy and found them all crying with the food in their hands. What he saw made him wonder: "How could the child give up his bicycle in exchange for a package of food for his family?"

The next day, Colonel Kanaan called the soldiers together, took up a collection and bought a new bicycle for the boy. They returned to the site to give that young boy his Christmas present. Both the family and the soldiers were very touched when they saw the happiness on the face of the boy when he received his brand-new bicycle. This event describes the spirit of humanity of the hundreds of soldiers who forgot for a moment their olive-green uniform and their rank in the Armed Forces to show dignity and respect for a refugee.

You may never have been in the presence of a refugee. But when you see the hopeful or hopeless look in the eyes of those who have fled across the border with nothing in their pockets - that is something that defies description. A refugee brings with him the uncertainty of starting a new life from scratch, and with deep scars in his soul from a past that, if it were possible, he would prefer to forget.

I have seen people leave Brazil to wander around Asia or hike through Europe, away from everything and everyone, in order to meditate on finding themselves and the purpose of life. I would advise anyone who suffers from anxiety, anguish or depression, and who is seeking balance and peace in their life, to spend a week visiting a refugee camp. Instead of spiritual affliction, they would go back home with a heart full of gratitude.

On another occasion, we went to meet the Mayor of the city, Teresa Surita. She explained that many local residents complained that their neighborhoods were degenerating, that they were now competing with Venezuelans for jobs and space in schools or doctor's appointments. She was aware that this immigration process would not soon go away. The impact on health care could be verified by looking at the maternity wards in the city, where there were 900 births per month and Venezuelan mothers accounted for almost one third of those births.

How does one cope with a new, unexpected, and unfamiliar reality? The Mayor need to find a solution for providing medical treatment and medications. In the area of education, classrooms must be provided for both Brazilian and Venezuelan children. After all, never before in the history of Brazil, had a small city, isolated from the rest of the country, been asked to take care of so many immigrants.

When we had been in Boa Vista for only ten days, we realized that during that period more than five thousand people had come across the border. Regarding that number of immigrants, the numbers are something like this: According to data furnished by the Federal Police, half of those people simply travel through the city and continue on to other Latin American countries. Around 200 persons already know where they are going in some state of Brazil, where they have a base of support, either a relative or a friend. How-ever, 50 people arrive in Boa Vista every day without a fixed destination, without any support, without reference, without food and without knowing where to go. Some are young, some are elderly. Some come with a family, others alone. Some arrive ill or with some special need. Many are single mothers with two or three little children. Those 50 persons per day are what are categorized as vulnerable. Those are the ones whom we saw crowded around the bus station, in the parks and public spaces in the hope of receiving some type of assistance as a miracle in their life. However, 50 people a day represent 1500 vulnerable people arriving in the city each month.

When confronted with this new reality, it was as if God said with a loud voice *Carlos, wake up! This is your mission!* It made me open my eyes to situations I had never experienced in my life. That is where I learned something about love, faith and hope. I was to learn more about life and starting over from scratch than I could have imagined. I was to learn from the Venezuelan immigrants just what courage means. Courage to flee from their homeland in search of hope.

At that moment, I also learned that this was not to be an isolated act. It was to be an effort of teamwork with partners and volunteers from various agencies from around the world in an effort to accommodate these people, to provide a moment of peace in their hearts and to feed their empty bellies.

At that time, Operation Goodwill, led by the Brazilian Army was beginning to take shape. The military men soon realized that they would need to coordinate efforts and not simply command. The verb "cooperate" became an integral part of their daily tasks from that moment on. The mission became a vast system of cooperation among agencies, both from civilians and from the military. The Army offered its hands to all who were involved and for the Operation to be successful it would be necessary to involve volunteers in all levels and to allow space at the decision table for all those who were willing to help.

The Operation's primary objective was to get the people off the streets, parks and bus station and provide basic food and suitable shelter. The building of shelters was then initiated in several locations in the city. In all, 12 gathering places were set up. Some with capacity to accommodate 500 refugees, others could house almost a thousand people. At those places, food was furnished daily and people slept in canvas army tents or in high-density fiber shelters made in Sweden especially designed for low temperatures and donated by the UN.

However, Boa Vista is just above the equator. It is one of the hottest places in Brazil. On a normal day, the temperature inside one of these shelters reaches more than 115°F. So, during the day, the temperature is unbearable. One fact, however, is indisputable: Refugees are unanimous in saying that they would rather suffer the heat of Boa Vista than to starve in Venezuela.

Operation Goodwill brought great relief to the immigrants and permanent residents of the city. When I arrived, prior to the setting up of these services, people were camped out in the parks. In fact, the main gathering place was Simon Bolivar square. I imagine they felt at home there. It was actually a deplorable scene that did not seem to have any solution. The number of people arriving multiplied each day and there was nowhere they could go.

Later, even with 12 shelters in the city, there was not enough space to shelter so many people. That is when an overnight area was created next to the bus station. It was not a proper shelter like the others, but was made up of Army bivouac tents, set up so that people would not sleep out in the open. Parents, women and children on one side and single men on the other side.

When night fell, churches and assistance groups would serve meals. To meet this continual influx of people outside of the shelters, a well-organized system was set up next to the bus station and thanks to the work of hundreds of volunteers, a lunch was served, consisting of rice and a mixture of nutrients. In order to be fed, you just needed to get in line with a pot.

In that situation, the refugees make do with what they have. If they don't have a plate, like most of the people, they just take a margarine or ice cream container, which is filled to the top to then be eaten. Seconds are given only after all have been fed (more than a thousand people). Incredible as it may seem, it is mostly the children who have seconds. Sometimes, two or three helpings for lunch. This may be because they know what hunger feels like and do not want that feeling again so soon. If you are a father or mother, you must understand what I am saying. Nothing compares with the worried look of these parents who stand in line to get food for their little ones.

I learned that some of the refugees spent months in the shelters. They were reduced to numbers. Only when they were called by their names did they recover their own identity and self-esteem. Some agents told me that there were plans to double the number of shelters in the city. With this information, my mind kept wondering, *How long is endless? How does one fill the daily monotony in a refugee camp? How does one face life without any hope for the future?* Boa Vista is not a destination. It is only the entryway. This state has no industries or large companies to offer employment, even for the local residents, let alone for the flood of immigrating refugees. A refugee has no chance for a job here.

All that seemed like a huge pressure cooker about to explode at any moment. It was chaos. My desire was to do something useful. I didn't know what or how, but I needed to begin to act. Seeing all those challenges at the start of my mission, I hadn't the slightest idea how to organize all that. I saw the challenge but I didn't yet see a solution.

I have always believed that when we don't know how to continue or where to start, we need to dedicate body and soul to find the solution or at least keep going until we see the light at the end of the tunnel. At these moments I learned to trust in the inspiration that comes from heaven.

One morning, I woke up and felt that I was incredibly in tune with the world and heaven. I felt a perfect connection between the implacable rational businessman in search of a solution and the human being whose heart had been troubled, impacted by the suffering of these people, and was at the same time seeking divine inspiration.

In that moment, I felt that this mission had awakened in me a humanity that I had thus far never had the opportunity to unveil or practice. It was now time to apply all the knowledge I had obtained through my life. It was more than a mission. It was a test. One of those that God administers to see if you have really learned all those things you have been preaching all your life.

Finally, the solution was right before my eyes. Of course, there were many obstacles to overcome before fully implementing it. That is what you will discover in the next few pages.

No one leaves home unless home is the mouth of a shark.

Warsan Shire

6

FOCUS ON THE SOLUTION, NOT ON THE PROBLEM

"Good morning, Jeff. My name is Carlos. This is my wife, Vânia. We arrived two weeks ago in Boa Vista with the mission to help Venezuelans who come to Brazil in search of shelter, safety and a better way of life."

At that time, Jeff Frederick was the chief representative of UNHCR (United Nations High Commissioner for Refugees). This tall Canadian from Toronto received us cordially in his office.

"And what are your plans? How do you intend to help? Do you have something in mind?" were the first questions.

"During the short time we have been here, it has become clear to us that the solution to the migratory influx from Venezuela is not found in Boa Vista. It is shared with the other states in the country, especially in the south, southeast and central west where the economy is strong and there are many job opportunities."

"So, how do you propose to accomplish settling these immigrants in other states?"

That was a logical question. I, however, didn't know the whole answer. I didn't yet have all my ducks in a row. I only had a vague idea of a possible solution.

"I am not connected to the government. I have no connection with NGOs. I am a business person and represent civilian society. Through my contacts with companies, community and religious leaders, I intend to create a large domestic program of relocation of these families who are seeking the chance for a new beginning in life."

He then asked me:

"In other words, your plan is to promote the relocation of refugees?"

Relocation of refugees. This was a new concept to me, but it would become my major objective, my goal, my purpose for the 20 months of my stay in Boa Vista.

"Exactly! Through organized civilian cooperation, we would like to become the largest partner in Operation Goodwill to promote relocation of refugees on a large scale."

He looked at me for a few moments and then said:

"Your idea sounds great. However, you have a big problem ahead of you."

I was anxious to hear what that was and he continued:

"The Amazon Forest! It separates Boa Vista from the rest of Brazil. How do you intend to transport all these people to the south of the country?"

Confident in the divine inspiration that has always guided me in important decisions, I only said:

"I think I have the solution, but I prefer not to tell you just now what it is. We can talk about that next week."

"O.K. Agreed. I will await your solution."

When I became involved with this humanitarian mission, I had no idea that it would impact so many lives, that it would change the destinies of so many families and that our work in Boa Vista would make a difference in the future of thousands of people.

As soon as we decided to act to aid those people who daily implored us for help, I understood that it was not enough just to use your heart. We needed a practical solution, not simply a palliative relief measure. Of course, we became aware of their dramatic stories, but we needed, above all, to act. To act in the effort to transform that entire situation and find solutions that would bring a real change in the lives of refugees.

It was time to use the businessman's attributes that I had developed. To use my intellect and my strategic capacity to provide a way out for that large number of refugees to start a new life. And the numbers were growing day by day.

In my search for a plausible solution to the question of transportation that Jeff Fredrick had mentioned, one name kept circulating in my mind: David Neeleman. Even so, I hesitated to contact him. I thought: *Would he understand? Would he come to my aid? Would he help? How should I approach him?*

David, whose parents are Americans, was born in São Paulo in 1959. Until he was 5 years old he was raised in Brazil. Afterwards, he moved to Utah with his family. At 19 years of age, he returned to Brazil as a missionary for the Church of Jesus Christ of Latter-day Saints. He spent 2 years in Brazilian territory serving the people. As an adult, Neeleman spent most of his professional life in the aviation world. As most people know. he is the founder of several airline companies such as Morris Air, WestJet, JetBlue and Azul Brazilian Airlines.

One of the personal characteristics of David is that he suffers from ADD. I knew that I couldn't take more than a minute to get his attention. And so, when I called him in Connecticut, I went straight to the point:

"Hello, David. I am in need of a favor from you."

"Very well, Carlos, how can I help?"

"I have been in Boa Vista now for a month. We will be spending 2 years here on a humanitarian mission receiving Venezuelan refugees. We need your help with airline transportation."

"Ah, I understand. You would like to purchase airfare at a discount."

His reaction was the logical reasoning of a businessman.

"Actually, no, David. I was thinking something different. Every day an Azul flight takes off from this city, I would like to know if you could offer vacant seats on those flights at no cost for Venezuelan refugees. If there is one vacant seat, I will use that seat. If there are five seats, I will use five. If there are none, no refugee will travel."

"How many seats do you suppose you would need under these conditions?" he asked.

Quite frankly, I don't know. I have just arrived here. But I can guarantee that every day we will have at least one passenger. The number, though, is not important, David. If you can offer a free flight for a single family each day, it will be a tremendous contribution to this humanitarian cause.

The answer that came then gave me hope.

"O.K., I'm in...on one condition."

"All right, tell me what it is."

"As long as the other airline companies also participate in this program."

That condition did not surprise me. Then I said:

"You are right. If I were in your place, I would say the same thing. If you agree, I would like to propose something, David. What if Azul goes first and shows support for the refugee cause, and after two months of operation, I go knock on the doors of Latam and Gol airlines?"

"Excellent. Let's do that. You may contact John Rodgerson, the CEO of Azul in São Paulo and we will give our support to this humanitarian cause."

After conversing with John, he immediately gave full support and committed to cooperate together with his team for the success of the program. Every day, his team in Boa Vista would inform us of any vacant seats on the flight. According to the available seats, Vânia and I would go to the shelters, load the refugees into our car and drive them to the airport. We expected to send one family per flight. Sometimes, however, Paulo, Azul's local manager would surprise us with the news:

"Carlos, tomorrow, you may bring 20 passengers. The flight is very much available."

With each family that left, there was a huge celebration. We took pictures, Vânia would prepare a small snack for each refugee, we would embrace and weep together to see them go for a new life. I shall never forget one particular family with three children. At check-in, the Azul agent told them:

"Please place your luggage on the scale."

I knew very well the reason for this instruction. Luggage could not go if it were overweight. The head of the family placed the "luggage" on the scale. All they had was a plastic bag weighing a few pounds of luggage.

Vânia and I were speechless as we witnessed that family who were leaving to begin a new life. They had fled from hunger in their country and all they had left was a plastic bag containing a few pounds baggage.

With daily departures, at this rate, we soon reached 100, 200, 300, 500 passengers. With each goal, we held a dinner with the Azul team. Sometimes it was a pizza. Sometimes, a lunch at the airport, or even taking the entire team to our house for a typical Brazilian "churrasco". We knew that each member of the team was important in this mission to assist and transport the refugees.

At the end of 60 days, I went to São Paulo to meet with the directors of the two other airline companies. Both were impressed by the magnitude of the mission, and sympathetic to the cause. They immediately agreed to participate in the program.

In 2019, out of nowhere came a phone call that threw me for a loop.

"Hello, Carlos. This is Claudio. I am one the directors of Gol Airlines and we are having a corporate governance audit. The auditors are asking us about the nature of the agreement for Venezuelans refugees, who are received by the Army in Boa Vista, who take advantage of the federal relocation program, being coordinated by Carlos Wizard, who has no legal ties with the government or with the Army. For the auditors, this relationship is not very clear and is not transparent. There is no official document that connects all the parts involved in the program."

My blood immediately ran cold. Now, what is going to happen? Will they cut off our program? Thinking of how to solve this, I asked:

"So, what do we need to do to solve this question, Mr. Claudio?"

"We will need to call a meeting of the three airlines, take this question to the federal government in Brasilia, Brazil's capital, and request the signature of an agreement by the National Aviation Association and the Army, granting approval of this free transportation for refugees."

Then, my mind filled with fear: Will the refugees be able to continue flying while this bureaucracy is being taken care of in Brasilia? I hesitated, but I asked:

"I understand that it is important to make this agreement official. But, in the meantime, this support program for the refugees will not be interrupted, will it?"

"No, of course not, Carlos. We do not want to discontinue the program, just to make it official. But there is one more detail."

"All right. Tell me what it is."

"Since this agreement does not have the seal of approval from the National Aviation Agency, from now on, you will have to pay the departure fee for each passenger."

"So, how much is the fee?"

"It will depend on the city of destination, but it varies between ten and twenty dollars per passenger."

Thank heavens. I sighed in relief. From that time forward, every night, as I took the refugees to the airport, I would stop by the travel office of each airline company to make the payment of the departure fee. Although I did not agree with it, I did not complain because I knew that the price of an airfare to the south of the country was not less than 400 dollars. Fortunately, Azul and Latam never charged us the departure fee. I believe that the auditors of these companies were not so demanding, or the airlines were more benevolent with regard to this fee.

I will not tell how many times I had to travel from Boa Vista to Brasilia for meetings with representatives of the companies and the federal government to make that agreement official. I knew that all the work we were doing depended on the good will and the signature of those authorities. It wasn't all that simple. Each company had its own interest at heart, its own legal department, and each clause needed to pass the review of several committees. After many comings and goings and an immense number of phone calls, in June of 2019, almost a full year after the beginning of the partnership, the agreement was finally signed in Brasilia. That same week, I read a note in the newspaper reporting that: "The federal government, sympathetic to the cause of Venezuelan refugees, promptly signed an agreement with airline companies to provide free transportation from Boa Vista to various cities of Brazil."

I thought to myself: *Good thing the agreement was signed promptly. Imagine if they had not been so prompt in signing.*

Finally, with that agreement formally signed by the government, I knew that the "relocation program" would pick up speed, since, in addition to the three airline companies, there were flights made by the Brazilian Air Force, which sporadically transported the immigrants.

Having solved the question of air transport, my mind returned to the conversation I had had with Jeff Frederick. Who would host the immigrants? The though kept bothering me. I always looked for solutions for the demands that arose, especially as to how to scale up the hosting program. One day I resolved to contact my friend Michael Aboud, who is a business person and a minister of an evangelical denomination. I began the conversation in this fashion:

"Hello, Michael. I know that you are one of the greatest business, community and religious leaders in the country. As you know, my wife and I are on a humanitarian mission in Boa Vista. And now we need your assistance."

His response was immediate:

"Are you needing food, clothing and medications for the refugees?"

"Yes, we are, but at this moment we have a different need."

He went straight to the point:

"What is your plan, Carlos?"

I explained that I would like to know if his church could host one or two families in his community.

"Just host? Is that all?" he asked.

"Well, hosting would include finding a house with affordable rent, up to 100 dollars, set up a campaign to gather household items, clothing and food."

"Who would pay the rent?"

"Hosting would include paying the rent for 2 months. Not only rent but the water and light bill as well."

"Ah, yes, I understand. Well, at this moment, I am at the airport, about to leave for New York. I promise to think about it. When I return, I would like to go to Boa Vista with my wife, Liana, to see close up the condition of the refugees."

"Since you are a religious man, I would like to share a Bible verse with you. I suggest you read Matthew 25:35-40. Have a good trip and I hope to hear from you soon."

I thought to myself: *Oh, no! This is going to be another case of people "sympathetic" to the refugees' cause with a promise to talk about it later. There are so many promises that do not materialize in practice. In the end, they usually fall by the wayside.*

To my surprise, a few weeks later I received a phone call:

"Hello, Carlos, this is Michael. I would like to inform you that Liana and I will arrive in Boa Vista next week. During the flight to New York, I read the verses of Matthew 25 several times and felt that this is a call from God. We will contribute to this humanitarian cause."

To make a long story short, Michael Aboud and his wife Liana stayed several days in Boa Vista, they visited the shelters, got to know the refugees, talked to the immigrants in the streets and at the bus station, and in the end, met with General Pazuello. They said:

"General, we will take 500 Venezuelan refugees to our city in the south of Brazil. We will offer lodging, food and clothing. And more importantly, we will give support to finding a place in the job market. You can reserve two Air Force flights, each one with 250 passengers. Our church will select a couple, who we will call an angel couple, to host each family as refugees arrive in our city.

Now, I want you to imagine the feelings instilled in the soul, heart and spirit of each person hosted by Pastor Aboud. They literally came from misery, off the street, from hunger and were met with a huge party and celebration offered by his organization. With emotion, both the hosted and the hosting families wept together. All this humanitarian effort was reported in prime-time on the country's major television networks.

Michael Aboud was an exemplary leader. His love surpassed even his own expectations. Not only did he host the refugees, but through his example and his legitimate love for the poor and needy, he inspired dozens of other religious leaders to do the same. In my heart, there will always be a special place of gratitude for this man of God, whom I learned to admire, for his spirit of solidarity and compassion for refugees.

To be called a refugee is the opposite of an insult; it is a badge of strength, courage, and victory.

Tennessee Office for Refugees

7

THIS WORK IS NOT YOURS

One day I was in the middle of a typical day in Boa Vista. One of those days when you have so many tasks that you don't know what to do first. As soon as you begin to do something important, something more urgent appears as well as other things that cannot be put off another day. There were people showing up at the border, people leaving Boa Vista, people being born and people dying, people asking for food and people asking for medication, people trying to get transportation, hosting, documents, vaccines. I literally didn't know who to help first.

At that moment, I looked up to heaven and thought:

Lord, will I ever be able to do this work?

I am always moved when I remember that almost audible voice, at the moment I most needed bolstering:

Calm down! Calm down, Carlos. This work is not yours. This work is Mine.

At that moment, I felt small in light of the magnitude of the work. That inspired answer accompanied me every day in the mission, giving me the peace and serenity I needed to do the best I could, but knowing that the final result was in God's hands.

There is a scripture that perfectly describes that feeling:

"Therefore, dearly beloved brethren, let us cheerfully do all things that lie in our power; and then may we stand still, with the utmost assurance, to see the salvation of God, and for his arm to be revealed." (Doctrines & Covenants 123:17)

The Bible tells the story of Moses who led his people from morning to night. On a certain day, his father-in-law, Jethro, gave him some advice, saying:

"What you are doing is not good. This way, you and your people will perish. Chose a few God-fearing men, some to officiate over thousands, hundreds, fifties and tens. Let them judge these people at all times, but have them bring the most difficult cases to you, but allow them to judge the minor cases. That will make your load lighter. If you do that, you will be able to stand the strain. And all these people will go home satisfied." (Exodus 18:17-23)

Inspired by Moses' story, I realized that I needed to delegate responsibilities among a larger team. The work was too heavy and the call was immense. I felt that I needed to connect with business, governmental and religious leaders, so that I might concentrate on the more strategic issues that would benefit the largest number of people.

I knew that Geraldo was giving all that he could as my assistant, but he was already working at near his limit. He was the type of person who spares no effort to support me and didn't know how to say no.

Born in the Amazon, he had considered becoming a priest when he was young, but had decided to marry once he found the woman of his life. Then when he became the father of two little girls, he proudly says he found the purpose of his life. Geraldo is very big-hearted. He would go to the hospital with Venezuelans so that they didn't have to go unaccompanied, and if necessary, he would stay the night with the patient because he couldn't bring himself to go home until he knew that everything was all right.

One time, when the engine of his old car was on its last legs, he went out on the road late at night, headed for a neighboring town. He was hoping to find a family of refugees with small children who were coming of foot because they didn't have the five dollars necessary to buy a bus ticket. By four in the morning, he hadn't found them so he stopped his car and said a prayer. Then he heard a voice and realized that there were people in the forest. He went in and found the family who had become lost. They were dehydrated, hungry and with blisters on their feet. He took them directly to the hospital. He had not slept for 24 hours, but he stayed up with them until noon the next day.

Geraldo has an unshakable faith in life. Whenever he feels like turning his back, he talks with God. "I converse with Him just like I am talking to you." he said. "Because He is my friend and I tell him what is going on and ask Him for advice. He always gives me direction."

So, that is how our partnering and friendship evolved and strengthened. Together, we resolved more issues than we could have imagined. It was obvious that we were not working with mere numbers. These were real people. And miracles came when we least expected them. However, even with all of Geraldo's support and consideration, we were unable to fully care for so many people who kept pouring in.

One day, my friend, Juraci Toledo, came to see me:

"I am moving away from this place. I can't find work here. I'm going back to the south. Would it be possible for my son, Pedro, to help you in your mission?"

I had a brief talk with Pedro and we hit it off right away. Compared with Geraldo, Pedro was more guided by his reasoning than by his heart. With the logical inclination of a person who develops strategies for doing things right and a transparent and honest character, typical of a family man, who will do whatever is possible to be the breadwinner for his family, he was ready to cooperate. But he seemed to know exactly where the fine line is between understanding other people's problems in order to help them, and bringing the problems home. He was a person who seemed to be able to solve any type of issue without being overly worried or carried away by emotions.

With the usual calm tone in his voice, he came right out and said:

"Before I start, Carlos, I need to tell you that there is a small problem."

"Go ahead, Pedro, Tell me what the small problem is."

That is when he seemed a little uneasy and said:

"I don't have a car. How can I help with taking refugees to the bus station, airport or hospital without a car?"

In my opinion, that was not a problem. It was something we could take care of. He needed a tool to work with.

"Don't worry, Pedro. We can work that out."

Coincidentally, that very week Geraldo came to me and said that the engine in his old car had just given up the ghost. I found myself with a problem that needed solving. Pedro without a car, Geraldo without a car. Now what would I do?

They were both very excited when I gave them the news:

"My friends, I am allocating a certain amount and each one of you will buy your car. When you find your car, let me know."

They both looked like children on Christmas morning. They immediately imagined driving the latest model imported pickup, with air conditioning and all the optional accessories like those used by the international agencies in

Boa Vista, with blue license plates. I could see in their eyes their disappointment when I added:

"Each of you have a budget of five thousand dollars to buy a used vw van."

As each one received that bucket of cold water in the face, they tried to conceal their disappointment. Pedro, who liked to argue, looked at me in a curious way and commented:

"But a vw van burns a lot of gas. It wouldn't have air conditioning. It gets really hot here in Boa Vista. It's hard to find an old vw van in good condition."

I knew that those arguments were valid. I also knew that I needed to wisely allocate resources for the mission. My answer, after some consideration was as follows:

"Pedro, I have learned two things in life: First, leaders do more with less. Second, read Matthew 7:7 'seek and ye shall find'. Go looking and you will find your vw van in good condition."

They looked at each other, divided between disappointment and hope, and went out to find the vehicles that would be with them from then on. After a few days, each one had found his vw van. The one that Geraldo bought had an inscription on the back that he insisted on keeping: "Missionary of Jesus".

As time passed, since our work intensified, I invited Pedro's wife to join our humanitarian cause. Queine was one of those congenial types, with a pleasing voice who cloned herself to take care of work, her child and her husband. She gave the utmost attention to everything. She loved to welcome people into her home and, in spite of the simplicity, she always offered the best of anything she had so that people felt at ease in her presence. She knew how to treat both refugees and people of the highest social class. She was a woman who personified an unmistakable calm under pressure, and I loved her commitment to the refugee cause.

Pedro and Queine together formed a perfect team. She spoke calmly, thinking about the best way to optimize things. Details were always uppermost in her mind. Pedro would readily take on a challenge with precision. He would solve everything and the problems would never be heard of again.

One day, Vânia and I went to the airport to accompany a family that was leaving. We said our goodbyes and took photos. We hugged and the family boarded the plane. We were leaving the airport when a young lady approached us:

"Are you Mr. Carlos Wizard?"

She looked young, talked fast, was enthusiastic and full of energy.

"Yes, that's me. What is your name?"

"I am Zizi. I have read your books, seen your videos and heard about your work with refugees here in Boa Vista. Congratulations."

Her eyes shone. She had a beautiful smile as if she were admiring me without any interest other than that of helping refugees.

"No need to congratulate me. This is a job that involves many hands. There are a number of military and voluntary agencies that participate in this humanitarian effort."

Her next question surprised me.

"Do you ever need more volunteers?"

Obviously, we did, but we had never been approached by people at the airport who wanted to help instead of wanting to get help.

"Actually, we do need lots of help. Would you like to become involved, too?"

Her answer was quick and to the point.

"Yes. I feel a definite connection with the refugee issue. Can we set a time to talk about it?"

"Yes, let's do that! We are here at the airport every day at this time. This is a good place for us to meet."

Often, people ask me where my office is, my headquarters, my workplace. I usually just say that it is at the airport. We have become acquainted with federal agents, taxi drivers and even the people that do the cleaning at the airport. The most meaningful moments of our mission have taken place there. That is the place where I developed some humility. Previously, in my corporate world, every time I would go on an international trip, the airline agent would be waiting for me at the airport. When she saw me, she would offer to carry my luggage. She would take me to the front of the line. I would be the first to be served and sometimes she would accompany me to the VIP lounge.

In Boa Vista, when I went to the airport, the process would be completely reversed. I would accompany the family of refugees and would wait at the end of the line. Then, when everyone else had been boarded, I would be the last to be served. In my heart there was always the hope that there would be seats available on the flight so that I could get one more family on board.

Some families waited weeks, others months for a chance to live that moment of departure. When they finally got a boarding pass in their hand, they would repeat the name of their destination over and over: Botucatu, Apucarana, Guaratingueta. They had never heard these names before. They didn't know for sure where these places were. It might be the first time they had ever boarded an airplane. In their heart there was only one hope: *Someone will be there waiting for me when I arrive. In that unknown place I will find employment. My children will be able to get an education. We will have a better future.*

It was normal for us as we awaited the departure time for each family to hear about their past and personal experiences in their lives. It was as though we had known them for a long time, as if we were truly family and now they wanted to share something special about themselves with us.

When boarding time came, after lots of photos, they would hug us, often in tears, full of gratitude. Each time we sent a new family off, we felt more love for the cause.

We felt that our impact in Boa Vista, with Operation Goodwill, was a positive one, that we were contributing so that new destinies were given to those refugees. We felt that we were motivated by God.

We said goodbye, Zizi left, and Vânia and I went to the Azul counter to check availability on the next day's flight.

All of a sudden, there was Zizi again. As she was walking to her car, she said that her inner voice talked to her: *Go back and tell them that you are going to help the refugee cause.*

"Here. I will give you my phone number. If we don't meet here at the airport, you can give me a call. I really want to help refugees."

Even though she didn't know exactly what we did, she still came back. At the time, I even thought that I wouldn't call her because I believed that many people offered help only to make contact with me for some business purpose.

That demonstration of genuine love for the cause moved me and that is how Zizi became part of our support team. She created a network of evangelical ministers, hosts for families in various parts of the country. Her reward was when she received photos of the families when they arrived at their destination showing the kids already in school.

Later on, she told me a little about her purpose in life. She and her husband, Rafael, did not have children. They lived in the outskirts of Boa Vista. The couple opened a little place in their backyard designed to offer education, food and clothing for needy children of the neighborhood. She does this with her own resources.

I was moved when she told me that when she feeds the children, she gives them chocolate milk, yogurt and juices. But they are always brand-name products. She gives the children the best available on the market. Zizi does not want them to feel that they are eating and drinking the cheapest thing on the supermarket shelves. She says that this is the only chance that those children have a chance to taste a brand-name product. This makes kids feel good, and made her feel good, too.

Examples like Zizi show how God always prepares people to carry out His work. As the mission gained momentum, no matter how much we felt that there was no more room for progress, we kept going and out of nowhere, like a miracle, some angel would appear as if sent from heaven to support us. At the end, the result always turned out better than if I had done the job myself.

No one puts their children in a boat unless the water is safer than the land.

Warsan Shire

8

ANGELS FROM GOD

When the media got wind of our presence in Boa Vista and learned about effort to assist refugees, our humanitarian activities became a news story in the local, national and international media. Somehow, my phone number crossed the border and arrived at the most distant locations of Venezuela.

I suddenly began getting calls morning, noon and night from Venezuelans seeking information about documentation, vaccines, transportation and requirements to participate in the assistance program. Some wanted information about medical treatment for a family member who needed surgery. Others wanted to know if they could bring their pet. I began to feel like I was working the whole day in a call center.

At first, I thought that I needed to change my phone number. But I then heard that inner voice speak louder: *Maybe this is the reason you are here. Could this be the purpose of your mission? How can you close your eye and cover your ears to desperate people who are starving?*

Down deep, I felt it my duty to answer every one of those calls. At the same time, I was worried that I might be encouraging immigrants to come to Brazil. That was never my intention. I had limited myself to serving only those who arrived on Brazilian soil. On the other hand, if I spent my time answering all the questions of those wanting to cross the border, I wouldn't get anything else done.

Once again, I had the confirmation that this work was not mine, but of God. Like angels sent down from heaven, three Venezuelan ladies who lived in Brazil, spontaneously volunteered and offered to answer those calls. They were Mariela, Virginia and Alana. My words are insufficient to express my gratitude to these marvelous women, who accepted each phone call that came in. They would give all necessary information regarding immigration papers and other details the refugees would need in preparation for their journey.

One day, the phone rang and the call was from Church headquarters in São Paulo.

"We are watching your work in Boa Vista. We have good news. We have just called a couple to help you in your mission. Brother and Sister Myrrha are retired and will be dedicating a year of voluntary service in the Amazon with you. They will soon arrive in Boa Vista".

This news came as music to our ears. We were anxious to meet them.

Alessandra had an immigrant history in her family. Her great-grandfather had come to Brazil as a refugee from Lebanon when he was 14 years old. Rodrigo's ancestors came from Italy in search of a better life in Brazil.

The couple could identify with the condition of the refugees. In 2007, they had gone to Santa Maria, in the south of Brazil, where they spent 3 years doing voluntary work on a mission. They were accustomed to serving.

Portuguese is the national language in Brazil. In 2018, the couple spent two months in Spain, taking intensive classes in Spanish. Their goal was to volunteer for a mission in a Spanish-speaking country. They were surprised when they got called to go to Boa Vista. They never imagined that they would speak Spanish all day in Boa Vista, since all the refugees spoke Spanish.

When Alessandra learned that they were to go to the border of Brazil and Venezuela, she wondered:

What will I ever do there?

And she heard the answer from deep inside.

You will care for people, just like you have always done.

Their goals in humanitarian aid were very clear: to alleviate the suffering of people and promote their self-sufficiency. At the same time, Rodrigo was sure that people's problems were their own. He used to say:

"People's problems are heavy, difficult, but they are theirs. They are not mine. When your child is sick, you get involved 100% emotionally. When there are thousands of needy people, you need to understand that the situation may be difficult, but that is someone else's problem. If you take on the pain of a thousand people, you are the one who will become ill. A person is only able to help if he or she sees the situation from outside. If you get tangled up inside, suffering like the other person, you will not be able to help anyone."

Even being aware that we are human beings, that we feel and become involved with everything, whenever he expressed this, we realized that sometimes remaining distant was essential to effectively contribute to solutions.

The two of them had different perspectives. Rodrigo was a rational man, with calmness in his eyes and transmitted the assurance that everything would work out, as he cared for details without the least distress. Alessandra, on the other hand, was the more enthusiastic half of the pair. She collaborated in every issue, involved herself in everything, and dedicated her time and energy as if everyone were part of her family. At every meeting we held, she was the first to set up rules and standards for participation in the refugees program. At times, we would joke that these rules were valid for 24 hours, until something unexpected happened.

Although she seemed stern, Alessandra was always correct in her explanations when she was talking to a group of Venezuelans about what they could expect as they began their journey. She was the one who gave them information about what life would be like in Brazil.

"I hope that your arrival in Boa Vista will be the bottom of the pit for you. And, if you do not have a positive attitude, this crisis will not pass." That is how she taught classes in self-sufficiency before the immigrants left Boa Vista.

The involvement of the Myrrha couple brought new dimensions to our work. Alessandra mobilized health professionals from several parts of Brazil who came to Boa Vista as volunteers. During the year, her medical team made more than 20 thousand consultations with refugees.

Rodrigo always said that each person on this humanitarian mission has his or her own talent and way of solving problems. "When you combine these talents, the efforts complement each other and we are able to help more people."

They completed a brilliant year of voluntary service in Boa Vista, and even before they left, we were already missing their intense sociability that we enjoyed during 12 months together.

Another of those angels on Earth was Ronilson, a Jesuit priest who was in Boa Vista acting under an inter-faith exchange program for the humanitarian crisis. A philosopher, having studied in several parts of the world, he spoke six languages and brought a surprising background and curriculum to the mission in Boa Vista.

Father Ronilson witnessed some of the saddest stories that took place in Boa Vista. With his vow of poverty and dedication to the refugees, he was present for more shocking incidents than he had ever imagined.

Since he aided some of the children who lived in the street, many of them turned up very ill, debilitated and malnourished. He did his best to be everywhere and to help everyone he could.

When he heard of Isabelita, a one-year-old baby who was stricken with pneumonia, living with her mother, he learned that they were living behind a gas station. In those circumstances, things happened at a frightening pace. The little girl had already been ill for days when they arrived at Boa Vista. Soon, she developed pneumonia and was taken to the Children's Hospital. However, the child's condition deteriorated day by day. She was not recovering.

One day father Ronilson got a phone call that deeply troubled him: "Father, could you come and give the little girl her last rites? Isabelita has died. We are now arranging for a casket for her."

A very few days later, he faced a similar situation. A refugee family arrived with a four-year-old boy who was already seriously weakened with pneumonia. The child's parents were hopeful that he might recover, but that did not happen.

"To see that mother wailing 'Wake up my son! Wake up my son!', as she looked upon his body in the casket was something that dismayed me. I was able to officiate the viewing but that image was shocking and I have never gotten it out of my memory."

Following these episodes that represented heartbreakingly painful moments, father Ronilson was present when Maria, an extremely poor woman arrived from Venezuela with her two nephews in tow. One day, as they were giving out soup to the refugees, she fainted while waiting in line before it was her turn. She was taken quickly to the hospital. Father Ronilson and some others were waiting for the doctor's report. Abruptly, the doctor came and gave the verdict:

"She is gone. She passed away. She died of inanition. She died of starvation."

"That was the worst day of my life. How could I witness a person die of hunger before my very eyes? From that day forth, I promised that I would do my utmost to never allow any person to go hungry."

In spite of being continually shocked with cases of people dying in his arms, father Ronilson likes to recall one episode in which his intervention had a positive result.

"I was once called to give extreme unction to a Venezuelan young man so that he could die in peace. When I arrived there, a Venezuelan doctor, who was not allowed to practice in Brazil, was at his bedside and told me that he was not allowed to practice medicine, but he informed me: 'Father, I feel this young man can survive.'"

The priest decided to take him to the local hospital in hopes of saving his life. Unfortunately, there was an order given - it is not known where the order came from - the attendant simply stated: "We have no space for Venezuelans."

Being upset, the priest requested that the order be given to him in writing. The attendant had either the audacity or naiveté to write it down, stamp it and give it to him.

"It was a license to kill. How can this be? We will not care for you because you are a foreigner. The young boy was dehydrated, malnourished, with diarrhea and hunger. I was dismayed by that. I put him in my car and we went to another hospital. There they charitably admitted him. Good gracious, on that same day, he walked out of the hospital, he recovered his life."

Father Ronilson is proud to say that after this incident that young man got a nickname. Wherever he goes he is called Lazarus. Indeed, that poor refugee left the shelter as a dead man, after the priest had been called to give him extreme unction, he returned walking, safe and sound.

As the number of refugees grew, so did the number of requests for air tickets from the airline companies. One day, one of the directors of Azul Airlines called me:

"Carlos, we have noticed that requests for airline tickets are increasing every day. From now on there will be a specific agent assigned to take care of the refugees. Her name is Cinthia. If you have any specific need, just talk to her directly."

Cinthia had worked for Azul for 9 years. When she was assigned to take care of reservations for refugees, she didn't quite understand what that meant. "I've been transferred so many times from department to department and now I am on the travel team, there must be some purpose." She would say, with emotion, whenever she recalled how she became involved with refugees.

When I began sending the first e-mails to her, requesting reservations, she thought that I was some agent of the Boa Vista airport. When she noticed that I was sending e-mails requesting tickets seven days a week, she began to wonder. She found it strange that an airport agent would be working there, with such dedication, Saturdays, Sundays and holidays. Although she was involved in the cause, she didn't know 'Carlos Wizard', as a business leader in the country. Finally, one day, she couldn't resist and asked:

"Excuse me sir, but don't you take time off on the week-end?"

I explained to her that our calling was for seven days a week, 24 hours a day. Quite often, it was on weekends that the highest number of seats were available on the flights. Once she understood my personal involvement in the cause, she became even more enthusiastic about the mission. She started to read my books and watch the videos with my lectures.

Being a Christian, she told me that at home, it was common for her, her husband, Dan, and her parents to pray that the refugees would arrive safely at their destination cities. Each reservation, each ticket issued, each route adjustment was made as though she were doing it for a member of her family. With the permission of the company, she began to take her laptop home on weekends and holidays. Sometimes, she would be connected after midnight, making reservations for some family who had missed a connection or whose flight had been cancelled.

I will never forget two situations that impressed me greatly. On one occasion, when she was traveling on vacation with her husband, she took the laptop in her baggage because she didn't feel comfortable interrupting reservations for the refugees. On another occasion, she needed to have surgery to remove her gallbladder. Even during her recovery period at home, she did not neglect her love for the refugees. Every day, she willingly issued reservations for each family that left Boa Vista. She liked to say, lovingly:

"I can't abandon my refugees. I cannot rest until they arrive at their destination city. No limitless black credit card exists that can pay for the feeling of satisfaction I have when participating in this humanitarian cause."

As I return home after almost 2 years, my heart is full of gratitude for having assisted more than 12 thousand refugees to begin a new life. However, I do not exaggerate in saying that the work was only possible thanks to the support of Azul Airline Company and to the continuous, tireless and unconditional support of that marvelous woman named Cinthia da Silva Ferro.

The example set by these marvelous people, truly angels of God on the earth, reminds me of a story which occurred during the Second World War. In a certain city, bombings severely damaged a statue of Jesus Christ. Following the war, specialists attempted to reconstruct the statue. However, the hands could not be repaired. The people of the city decided to leave the statue without hands and placed a plaque at the base of the statue, which read: "You are my hands".

9

FROM BOA VISTA TO BRASILIA

I've never imagined that a humanitarian mission in the far north of the country, on the border with Venezuela, taking care of refugees, would put me so much in contact with government authorities, cabinet members, the President of the country and the First Lady. I represented organized civilian society, without any government ties. Even so, I was given free access to Brasilia, with the responsability to gain support for the refugees' cause.

Each time I traveled to Brazil's capital, I went with a schedule full of meetings. On one occasion, my friend Michael Aboud accompanied me to Brasilia. We had an appointment with Minister Damares Alves, a Cabinet Minister responsible for issues pertaining to Women, Family, and Human Rights. Mr. Aboud began the discussion with:

"Madam Minister, we are very much in need of your support. We are aware of your commitment to Human Rights, the defense of women and the family. Now, we are going through an unprecedented crisis in Boa Vista. 500 people cross the border each day."

The minister, who had a lineup of people at her office door waiting to see her, quickly asked:

"Mr. Aboud, what do you expect me to do?"

"My friend, Carlos Wizard left his companies, his business and his family in São Paulo to spend 2 years on the border, giving aid to the refugees. I will let him explain."

"Well, Madam Minister Damares, there are 70 thousand churches officially registered in Brazil. I believe that if only 10% of those churches hosted a single family, we would empty all refugee shelters on the border. Besides, churches, by their very nature, are goodwill organizations, concerned with the poor, the needy and the oppressed. This type of help is part of the gospel."

She listened to our explanation and responded with questions:

"So, what are you thinking about?"

"Well, since you are a member of the Evangelical movement in the country, oriented toward social causes, we would like to count on your support in making people aware, inviting religious leaders to participate in a national refugee program to assist Venezuelan that arrive in Brazil."

At that moment, I could see Mrs. Damares' eyes begin to shine. She smiled broadly, and I could feel that her heart connected with the refugee cause. She then invited her staff to make a list of the most influential religious leaders in the country.

In the weeks that followed, dozens of pastors nationwide, sympathetic to the cause of the refugees, decided to participate in the program. Each of them agreed to host many immigrant families in their congregations.

These religious leaders inspired many other denominations to follow their example of charity. If I were to cite all the religious leaders who made a difference in hosting one family, there would be no space to describe the goodness, generosity and self-sacrifice of all those who became good Samaritans. However, I will mention just one case that represents the charity of all those who embraced this cause of altruism.

At one particular moment, Operation Goodwill had invited a group of ten pastors to come to Boa Vista to see, up close, the refugee situation. One night, we went to visit an unauthorized occupation of a public building. We went to a building where the former State Education Department had once operated, and which was abandoned but now fully occupied by refugees.

For you to better understand the precarious conditions of the locale that we went to visit, you should imagine a scene from a war movie where there had been an air attack on those facilities. That is what we saw. It was total devastation: fractured, crumbling walls, more than 50 rooms or cubicles without ceilings. On the grounds among the ruins there was garbage, rubble and open sewage. There resided over 400 refugees, of which 180 were children. It was difficult to hold back the tears. One woman from Rio de Janeiro, who stood beside me, was fighting to hold back her tears and, speaking with trembling voice, didn't want to believe what she was seeing. People were piled into tiny spaces, women were building fire on the floor to heat up soup or some mush to feed their little children. It was pitch dark. In the midst of that gloomy scene, Reverend Jose Domingos from Rio de Janeiro stepped forward:

"These people are our brothers and sisters. We cannot leave them in these sub-human conditions. We must host them. Give me the largest family here. I will take them into my congregation."

Then, one of the local residents led us through a labyrinth. We passed from one place to another, from one environment to another and the more we penetrated into that inhospitable place, the more shocked we became.

Finally, we came to a cubicle where there was a woman named Maria, sitting on a bed.

"Maria, would you like to get out of this place?"

"Goodness gracious. I would like nothing more."

"Where is your husband?"

Someone ran to get Luis, Maria's husband.

"Do you have children?"

"Yes, I do?"

Suddenly, a whole brood of children began to climb onto the bed as if they were kittens around their mother cat. One, two, three, four, five, six, seven children; all of them barefooted, almost naked.

"Congratulations Maria. You have seven children, do you?"

"Yes, there are seven children, and I am pregnant with the eighth."

Soon, the father arrived, a bit awkward and a little proud of his numerous family.

"Luis, how long have you been here?" asked the Reverend.

"For almost a year. We have suffered much, we have gone hungry. We want to get out of here."

"Well, then, you can thank heaven. You will go to the most beautiful city in Brazil: Rio de Janeiro. There you will have a home, food, work and school for your children. You may pack your suitcases."

They all swelled with joy and then Luis said:

"Suitcases, Reverend? We have only some grocery bags."

Before the shock of such poverty could wear off, a crowd of people gathered around that cubicle. Suddenly, another refugee asked:

"What about my family, Reverend? Can we go, too? I am married. This is my wife and these are my children."

With unbridled generosity, pastor Jose announced:

"O.K. You will go with us as well".

As Reverend Jose Domingos prepared to take a photo together with the two families, a third appeared, pleading to be hosted. With a heart as big as all outdoors, he said:

"I came here willing to take one family. But I will take ten. The first three may come immediately. The others I will need some time to get things arranged first."

82

The visit of those pastors that night was permanently fixed in the mind of those people. A mircle began to happen among those abandoned refugees. It was an action that was to bring wonderful blessings to a great number of families from that community of unassisted and vulnerable refugees.

A few weeks later, I was received in Brasilia by the First Lady, Michelle Bolsonaro, President of the National Council of Volunteers. She promised to support the refugee cause. She recorded institutional videos inviting religious and business leaders to host refugee families in several parts of the country.

Some people, upon seeing my involvement with government authorities, have said in a skeptical tone: "That Carlos is a smart guy. He came to Boa Vista disguised as a missionary, and with money in his pocket, is carrying out social activities with his sights on a future political campaign. Maybe he plans to run for the senate, or city mayor...who knows, maybe governor of the state."

As a matter of fact, I have been invited to run for all of those posts, but my only objective in spending 2 years in Boa Vista was to answer a call from God to aid the refugees that have fled there. I have never imagined to use that altruistic work as a springboard to run for public office.

**Refugees are not terrorists.
They are often the first victims
of terrorism.**

António Manuel Guterres

10

PREPARING FOR A TRIP

One time, my six-year-old granddaughter Isabella, Priscila's daughter, was talking with her paternal grandfather. Grandpa Renato, a lawyer, was trying to explain to her what was needed to prepare for an overseas trip.

"First off, Isabella, you need to choose your destination. Then you do some research about the tourist attractions in that place. Then you need to find a travel agency or, if you prefer, you can look online for sites that sell tickets. Depending on the country where you will be going, you may need to get a passport. To do that, you will need to set up a date to take the necessary documents. Some countries require visas. Others don't. Once you have all these things done, the family is ready to go on the trip."

While her grandfather was explaining in detail all this process, Isabella was taking in every word. She heard her grandfather explain everything and just imagined her trip overseas. She imagined herself in the parks, playing with her cousins, eating ice cream, eating popcorn. In her imagination, she had already arrived at her destination and her thoughts were everywhere except on what he was telling her about all the paperwork, which meant nothing to her. Finally, her grandfather decided to test his granddaughter's memory and understanding:

"So, Isabella, tell me now, what is needed to take a trip overseas?"

"It's simple, grandpa. You pack your bags, go to the airport, get on the plane and take off."

In my simplistic way of figuring out the preparations for the refugees' trips, I often remembered Isabella's simple reasoning and would make the following comparison. Imagine that you are going to take an automobile trip. The car will comfortably fit five passengers. Someone suggests that with some small adjustments, it could take seven passengers. Then someone else says that since the trip will be long, we need a team to check the tires, another team to verify the condition of the engine, another to check the electrical system, another to check that the air conditioning is working perfectly. And we mustn't forget the brakes. While all these things are being checked, days and weeks, even months go by, and the car just sits there.

I use this example to explain my impatience with the weekly coordination meetings, where tens of agencies participate, each one with its own specific focus. Some cared for children, others for single mothers, others for the elderly, others for indigenous people, others for special needs, others for the LGBT community.

Of course, it is important to take care of each of these groups. I am in no way diminishing their importance. I just know that spending energy and resources in a continuous welfare program, without a vision for the future, was not the solution. To persist in this route meant to perpetuate the model that caused the dependency of the population and the consequent destruction of our neighbor to the north.

I heard many Venezuelans say:

"If we stay in a refugee camp for too long, it is like being prisoners, unable to go out and seek our own support. I want to do some kind of work, buy things for my family to cook, buy diapers for my child and not become dependent. It was the welfare programs in Venezuela that destroyed our country."

One morning, impatient with the sluggishness of the process, delays with federal agencies and departments, with their endless protocols to be followed so that the immigrants could get out of that "prison" called a refugee camp and continue on their course, I went to see Colonel Kanaan.

"My friend, Kanaan, you know me. I am not here for any personal, commercial or political gain. For more than a year, my wife and I have been here in this refugee cause. During this period, we have assisted more than 6 thousand people to get away from Boa Vista. Be frank with me. Do the Armed Forces really want to have our support? I am a very practical person, with focus on results. I feel that I could contribute more to the refugee cause. But, if you feel that we are just getting in the way or causing problems, please tell us."

"Oh, no, Carlos! We have great respect, fondness and admiration for you, your wife and the work you are doing. We wish we had more people like you acting as volunteers! You have full latitude to act and to support us in whatever is needed. We are together on this!"

That conversation motivated me to forge ahead and be more assertive in my ideas. I will never forget the silence that I provoked in one of the coordination meetings, when, after three hours of discussion, the person conducting the meeting asked:

"O.K. guys, our time is far spent. Let's close the meeting. Is there anything more that needs to be covered?"

That is when I couldn't resist any more and made my point.

"Excuse me, sir, I have a question. I'd like to know if there is a specific goal with the number of refugees to travel this month, how many immigrants have already left and how many are lacking to meet the goal."

This question produced an absolute silence in the room of about 50 people. That is, I knew then that there was no goal. No one knew how many people had been put into the program and what would be the result at the end of the month.

In light of that fact, it was clear that it was urgently necessary to review the concept, the model and the direction of the entire program, if we were to assist a large number of refugees to begin a new life. The operation seemed to be satisfying the initial requirements, that is, get people off the streets and into the shelters. At that moment, however, with 12 shelters totally filled up in the city, it seemed that the focus on the solution had been lost and that the operation had turned into a welfare action for immigrants. It was time to change the course of the operation.

I knew that it was all a matter of objective and purpose. Although while people were being aided, the impression was that everything was good, but in reality, it wasn't. I found out that some people had been in the camps for up to a year, getting three meals a day, medication, doctors' visits and security 24 hours a day. So, many were settling in and not looking to start an independent life.

With this thought in mind, I sent a message to an official close to the President of the country saying:

"Dear Secretary, would it be possible to meet this week to discuss the issue of refugees and how to streamline this process? If we do not take prompt measures, I fear that a tragedy may occur here in Boa Vista."

Within five minutes, I received the following answer:

"Come to Brasilia. You may schedule a meeting with my secretary."

So, the challenge was to use reason and logic, knowing that the Secretary had the power in his hands to take emergency measures to aid the refugees.

On the appointed day, I presented to the Secretary and his staff a plan of action to expand the refugee program, the objective of which was to protect the image of the Armed Forces, of the federal government, of the President of the country, and of the people of Boa Vista and, of course, to offer the greatest number of immigrants the opportunity to start a new life. For this to happen, we would need government support to increase the number of flights leaving the border region.

Today, I am thankful for the immediate support we got. Besides having more Air Force flights, we got to have more chartered flights to various cities in Brazil. Transportation of immigrants over land to Manaus became more frequent. Many time refugees where transported to Manaus by the military and from there they flew with airline companies.

During the last few months of my activities in Boa Vista, I had the pleasure of working side by side with General Barros. His priority was to accelerate the process of travel of the refugees. His initial goal was bold: he wanted to help three thousand refugees travel each month. With that objective in mind, I became his number one ally.

At that time Boa Vista faced two situations. About seven thousand refugees were accommodated in 12 shelters organized by the Army, UN and other agencies. And also there were thousands of refugees occupying abandoned buildings in the city.

In a certain way, General Barros and I were very well aligned, since he also had a focus on the refugees who were occupying these unsafe buildings. There were over 10 public buildings in Boa Vista that had been taken over by refugees when there was no room for them in the refugee camps.

The Armed Forces had a team of 500 trained, prepared and qualified personnel. In addition, more than 100 agencies collaborated in the refugee cause. What lots of people could not understand was how all those people with millions of dollars in their budget usually assisted two thousand refugees to travel per month, while my team of two persons, without structure, without a budget, was able to help an average of one thousand people to travel each month.

One day, I decided to shock my work companions, Geraldo and Pedro. I invited them to visit two of those occupied government buildings. Pedro, who was always questioning things, came out and asked:

"What are we going to do there, Carlos. Will we be taking food to the refugees?"

"Of course not, Pedro. We have been together for almost 2 years and you still don't understand what our goal is."

"You mean, you are thinking about ..."

"That's right, Pedro, I'm thinking about relocation. We need to help these refugees start a new life. But not here!"

"And where do you intend on sending these refugees?"

"Hang in there, my friend. You will see soon enough."

We started by visiting the first location. Imagine a huge warehouse with a great number of rooms and narrow corridors without lights. The image would be like a prison, so claustrophobic was the feeling it gave us. The walls, painted in dark colors increased the feeling of suffocation. There were about 400 refugees there, half of which were children. It had the name Happy Children. The only thing happy there was the name.

As soon as we arrived, we were surrounded by a huge crowd of people. They wanted to know what news we were bringing. I began:

"Attention everyone, who wants to get out of here and go to some other state in Brazil?"

Almost everyone raised their hand.

"We want to know who has a relative, friend or acquaintance or a job offer in another part of Brazil. Whoever can meet one of these conditions may leave tomorrow."

With this, people began to raise their hand, saying that they had a place to go in some other state in the country.

"My friends, Geraldo and Pedro, now you have an important task. Write down the names of all these people, verify their documents, vaccines and their host's contact information. Then verify if the host is really able to receive the family. If the result is positive, tomorrow we will bring a bus, take them directly to the airport in Manaus. And from there, they will depart for a new life."

By the end of the day, they had enough names to fill a bus with 50 passengers. The next day, we did the same thing at that dark location that was described in the previous chapter with the Reverend. We filled one more bus with 50 people. The local media got wind of our activity in favor of those unassisted and vulnerable refugees. The local TV station went to the locale to follow and document the departure of the first immigrants to be aided from those locations.

Pleased with the numbers they had reached, my two assistants came to me smiling:

"Mission accomplished, Chief!"

"What do you mean by 'mission accomplished'? Have you emptied all the places where there are refugees in the city?"

"Well, we went to the two places that you indicated. The rest of the people don't have their documents and vaccines up to date, or they don't have anyone to host them."

"Then, what are you going to do?"

"Just wait for them to get things ready."

"I can't believe it. It seems like you work for those refugee agencies who sit around waiting, and waiting...waiting for processes that go nowhere. No, my friends. That will not do!"

"What do you want from us now? Do you want to send us to other abandoned public buildings?"

"This very week, I went to Brasilia and met with General Barros, who just assumed command of the troops. He has a goal of assisting three thousand immigrants per month to leave Boa Vista. He is counting on our contribution of one thousand refugees. We are in the last week of January. We need 600 more people to reach the General's goal."

"Hold on, Carlos! We have a team of only two people. The army has more than 500 soldiers. Altogether, there are 100 agencies. Now, you want us two to find more than 600 persons to travel in less than a week?"

"Yes! That is exactly what I expect of you!"

"But where are we going to find so many people in so few days?"

"You two know where the bus station is in Boa Vista, right? So then, every day at noon, thousands of refugees crowd around that place to get a plate of food. Tomorrow, I want you two to go to that place and repeat the same procedure we used at the abandoned public buildings. You will be surprised with the results."

This time, it was Geraldo who piped up.

"I heard that there are soldiers and agency personnel who control that food distribution location. What is going to happen if they start to question us about what we are doing?"

"You will be prepared, Geraldo. They will question you."

"What should we say, then?"

"You can tell them that General Barros gave you an important mission to assist refugees leave Boa Vista and that you are working to comply with the General's orders."

And that is how Geraldo and Pedro rigorously obeyed the orientation I gave them.

The next day I was not in town, but I was very happy to receive a message from Pedro on my cellular phone.

"Carlos, you will never believe this. Everything you said actually happened. We have enough people to fill some ten buses."

In fact, the only ones who were surprised were those two. I have always held to the belief that fully a third of the immigrants who are in Boa Vista have a contact point somewhere else in the country. The only reason they do not move on is the red tape and the long processes. Of course, there is also the inertia on the part of some people. Pedro then continued with his description.

"When we arrived at noon at the bus station, there were over a thousand people standing in line, waiting to get their plate of food. When we started to invite people to be part of the travel program, that created a great commotion. For a moment, people forgot about their hunger and surrounded us, wanting details. It happened just as you said it would. Right away, a soldier came to question us:"

"Who are you? What are you doing here?"

"We work with relocation of refugees. We are following orders from General Barros." When they heard that answer, we suddenly had tables and chairs. They offered us water, juice, coffee, cookies. They made themselves available to help.

I will forever cherish and remember that experience. Before the end of the month, we had helped more than 800 people to leave Boa Vista, coming from the unauthorized occupations and from the lunch line at the bus station. Later on, the colonels in charge of the refugee program recognized the value of the work carried out by Geraldo and Pedro in their efforts with the most vulnerable refugees.

Someone is bound to ask what happened with General Barros' goal. We ended the month of January, 2020 with 3250 people in the travel program. Obviously, the general was very pleased. He had just assumed command and was already beating his own goal. The month of February immediately followed and one military man said to me:

"This month it will be impossible to put three thousand refugees in the program."

"Why would you say that?" I asked.

"You know. This is a short month. Besides, in Brazil we have Carnival. This is our big national holiday. You know what the Brazilian culture is like. No one does anything during the week of Carnival."

I didn't accept that negative forecast about the month that had just begun. With all respect for that officer, I simply responded:

"I don't know what the 500 military personnel and the tens of agencies will be doing in February. But this month, my team of two people will assist more than a thousand refugees to participate in the program."

He looked at me with an expression of someone who is thinking: "This guy is really crazy!"

That same day, I called Geraldo and Pedro.

"My friends, congratulations on the great results in January. However, in February, you are going to break that record. The goal this month is to exceed one thousand refugees in the travel program. Are you up to it?"

They both agreed and I promised them a special celebration for them and their wives at the end of the month. It is incredible what a little incentive and recognition can do to motivate people to exceed their limits. On the 29th of February, I was in São Paulo accompanying my wife who underwent a small surgery, when I received this message from Pedro:

"Do you remember the goal of a thousand people by the end of February? We have already passed our goal. We ended the month with 1386 refugees in the program. Most of those people came from the abandoned buildings and the bus station."

That experience reminds me of a concept I frequently used in the corporate world: "A person will rarely go beyond his own expectations." If they hadn't been challenged, perhaps they would not have obtained such good results.

In the final months that I spent in Boa Vista, each time I visited those illegal occupations, I had the feeling of a mission accomplished. I knew the people there by name, and I noticed that I was recognized for who I was and not for what I had acquired. No one in that inhospitable place knew who Carlos Wizard was. The greatest legacy that I can leave for my children is to be able to go into a place with my head held high, even though in those poor conditions no one knew how much money I had in my bank account or my net worth or the names of my companies. To be welcomed with a smile, a look of hope, a hug, a genuine desire to have an spontaneous conversation with a refugee to me was the greatest reward.

Refugees didn't just escape a place. They had to escape a thousand memories until they'd put enough time and distance between them and their misery to wake to a better day.

Nadia Hashimi

11

WHERE DO WE GO FROM HERE?

One of the most moving experiences of our humanitarian mission was the moment when each family arrived at the refugee camp in Boa Vista. I always tried to get to know something about their story, their decision to leave everything behind and depart for the unknown. Sometimes, we would sit under a shady tree in a more private place. The whole family would gather: father, mother, children, sometimes grandparents, sometimes other relatives. Each family brought their own story of suffering and anguish. They brought a pain that was not forgotten nor could it be ignored. The sacrifice of their long voyage was visible on each face, the weary journey and the dangers they face along the way.

After hearing the story from the adults, my attention turned to the children. I wanted them to feel part of such a memorable a moment. I would ask them what grade in school they were in. For the smaller ones I would ask them to count the numbers. I would normally ask them if they were afraid to get on an airplane. Then I would say:

"No need to be afraid. If you become afraid of getting on the plane, all you need to do is close your eyes and say a prayer. The fear will immediately go away."

A few days later, when I went to the airport with the family, before they boarded, I asked the little ones:

"What do you need to do if you become afraid?"

I would get emotional when they answered exactly: "Close my eyes and say a prayer."

Following the initial welcome contact with refugees, they almost always asked the same question:

"Where do we go from here, brother Martins?"

I would give the same answer to everyone.

"We have dozens of cities with hosts awaiting the arrival of a Venezuelan family. But it doesn't matter where you go. I am convinced in my heart that God knows you, and He has prepared the way so that you will be able to move forward, working, studying, progressing and serving your fellow beings with self-sufficiency and dignity."

Given the fact that over about 2 years of the mission, we assisted more than 12 thousand refugees, I had this experience at least three thousand times. There isn't enough paper to describe the emotion I felt at each of those moments. I will only mention a few of these experiences which I will never forget.

One night, while interviewing a family with father, mother and one daughter, the woman said that she was in need of a special medical treatment.

"Brother Martins, I have a particular health condition. What city would you recommend?"

"What is your health condition?"

"I have thyroid cancer."

I took a deep breath and asked them to give me some time before I could give them an answer. I returned home that evening knowing one thing for sure. I would need divine inspiration to find the most appropriate city to host this family. Vânia suggested that we send the family to the city of Barretos, near São Paulo, where there is one of the largest oncological treatment centers in Brazil. I phoned the Church leader in Barretos. I explained the situation and asked if they could host the family. The answer:

"Yes, we can host the family! However, we do not yet have a house ready. We still need to find the house, negotiate the rent, sign a contract, hold a campaign in the community to collect household articles, clothing, food, etc. I think that in two or three weeks we will have everything ready."

Although I thought that was a long time, I agreed:

"O.K., that sounds good. May I call you within a week or so to ask about the house?"

"Yes, feel free. You can call me any time."

Each time I called I was more nervous to learn that they had not yet found a house. After ten days, I started to doubt that the family should go to the city of Barretos. That is when I took the list of cities where we had hosts available and houses ready and began to seek some inspiration. I didn't know where to start. I looked at the list over and over and wondered:

How would I know? - Who should I talk to? - Maybe I should call every one of these cities until I find support. For some reason, I felt prompted to call the city of Joinville, in the state of Santa Catarina.

"Good evening. Is this Brother Euzebio?"

"Yes, that's me." Responded the voice on the other end of the line.

"I am calling from Boa Vista. We have just received a family from Venezuela. I would like to know, if by any chance there is a hospital in Joinville that specializes in cancer treatments?"

I had hardly finished speaking and he answered:

"In fact, we have two oncology centers; one public and the other private."

"The reason I am asking is that we have received a family and the wife is in need of a cancer treatment."

"Do you know what type of cancer she has?" he asked.

I told him that it was thyroid cancer and he then said:

"Well, you called the right place! My wife had cancer and had surgery here, took the treatment and is doing well. We have a member of the Church here in Joinville who had thyroid cancer. Both of them have been cured."

Upon receiving that happy answer, I was overjoyed.

"What wonderful news, Brother Euzebio. May we send the family to your city?"

His welcoming attitude was beyond belief.

"Yes, you may. We will receive them and take good care of them. In fact, there is a member of the Church here who is a doctor who works at the city hospital. We will give this lady every support she needs and deserves."

When I hung up the phone, it was difficult to contain my tears, because once again, I had the confirmation that "this was not my work but the work of God. And above all, He was directing the destiny of each of those refugees. What was even more strange was what happened the next day when I received a call. Can you guess from where? That is right. From Barretos.

"Good morning, Carlos. We finally found a house. You may send the family here."

I thanked him and explained the situation. The family was on their way to Joinville.

One day Vânia heard that a visually impaired man had arrived in Boa Vista carrying a one-year-old girl. According to what she had heard, the man was living on the street and was a member of the Church of Jesus Christ of Latter-day Saints.

This bit of news got Vania's attention and she couldn't get it out of her mind. No one knew where this visually impaired refugee was staying. She wondered what she could do to find this man and his little child.

After a few days, she went to take some medications to one of the city shelters, where there were more than 600 refugees. As she was leaving, an employee who was with her said:

"You know, Vânia, this week a visually impaired man with a child in his arms came here. I think he is a member of your Church."

This surprising news stirred her emotions. Her heart raced.

"Where are they now?" she asked.

"I think they are at the outpatient clinic." Was the answer.

"I need to talk to this man." Vânia said, anxiously.

"Do you know them?"

"No, I don't know them." she answered. "But I had heard that they had arrived in town."

They walked together to the outpatient clinic and Vania's heart seemed to race with emotion because she felt she needed to find this father and his child.

"Good morning. My name is Vânia and I am on a humanitarian mission here in Boa Vista. What is your name?"

"My name is Eduarto Vilanueva and this is my little daughter, Carley."

Vânia asked him where the mother was and the man hesitated for a moment, as though he did not want to speak and then he asked:

"Are you a member of the Church, too?"

"Yes, my husband and I are missionaries of the Church. Please tell me, brother Villanueva, I would like to know how we can help you."

He then hung his head and said, slowly:

"I have no wife now. Before we came to Brazil, we lived in Colombia. We fled the hunger in Venezuela. While we were in Colombia something terrible happened. One day a car ran over my wife. She died in the accident. As a consequence, I lost my 2-year-old son. The legal system in Colombia determined that I was not capable of caring for him. The boy was left with his maternal grandparents. All I have left now is my daughter, Carley. After that tragedy, we came to Brazil.

Vânia was shocked by this story. The image of the woman being struck by the car, the funeral, that husband's suffering from losing his wife and two-year-old son left her speechless for a few moments then she continued:

"Well, Brother Villanueva, I am deeply sorry for all the pain and anguish you have gone through. I'm not sure how we can help you, but God knows. We will pray for guidance and inspiration."

Vânia left the shelter that day with a lump in her throat. By that time, we had attended to over three thousand people, finding work, housing, and school for their children. But how could we help a visually impaired father with a one-year-old daughter?

Her greatest worry was the safety of the child. There were gangs in the city who approached young Venezuelan single mothers with the intention of kidnapping their babies. Imagine the risk to a child whose father is visually impaired.

While Vânia was seeking inspiration to find a solution, every day we would go the camp to visit our friend Villanueva. One day, we found him sleeping on a mattress inside the tent while his baby was playing by herself. Vania's fears only intensified. "This child could be kidnapped at any moment." she thought with concern.

The next day, we asked him if he needed something. He first said that he didn't need anything. He only asked for a few diapers for the little girl. The poverty of that father in that tent was obvious. I persisted in asking if he didn't need something. A little embarrassed, he said:

"You know, Brother Maritins, over the last few months, I have lost a good deal of weight. My pants keep falling down. If you could arrange a belt to hold my pants up, I would be very thankful. That same day, we took a belt and a few articles of clothing to him."

The next day, when we returned to visit him, Vania's preoccupation with the child's safety increased even more when Eduardo said.

"You don't know what happened yesterday. Last night, while I was sleeping, some thief came into our tent."

Vania's heart froze.

"He stole my belt."

At that moment, Vânia opened her heart and shared with Eduardo her greatest fear; the possible kidnapping of his daughter. Trying to find the right words, she decided to ask him:

"Brother Villanueva, sometimes I wake up at night, thinking about how to help you and how to protect your daughter. Please, don't misunderstand me. It is only a question. But have you ever, at any time, considered the possibility of putting your daughter up for adoption?"

With a trembling voice, he answered:

"Sister Vânia, you know that I am a member of the Church. All my life, I have obeyed the commandments of God. For some reason, God took my wife from me. He also took from me my two-year-old son. All I have left today is my one-year-old daughter. Do you think that I would give to someone else the only thing I have left? If I give her up for adoption, I will have nothing left."

There was nothing more to be said. We hugged, we wept. We could feel the supreme love from a father to his daughter. He could not imagine losing what was most precious in his life. And as we faced that man, who has such love for his daughter, we were sure that he would be strengthened by God to be able to care for her.

As we left the shelter, one thing was clear. We were not dealing with any common man. We had in front of us someone with courage, determination and irreproachable character, with a mature concept of family. Here was a man full of faith who knew what had been taken from him, even his sight, but he would not relinquish the most precious gift that had been given him.

This feeling was again confirmed the next day when we asked him how he managed to take care of himself with his visual limitation. Without hesitation, he responded:

"I have a profession. I am a street vendor. I have never depended on anyone else to make a living."

At that moment, I recalled the many people whose eyesight is perfect who complain about life, shifting the responsibility of earning a living to others. That day Eduardo taught me that he did not see life with his eyes, but he saw it with his soul.

In her search to find hosting for this loving father and his daughter, one day Vânia phoned a friend of hers by the name of Alba. After hearing the explanation of the situation, Alba answered:

"Vânia, I know of a relief institution in the city of Jatai, in inland of Brazil, whose founder is a doctor. He and his wife Zelia are dedicated to helping people with special needs. I will give them a call and get back to you."

That same day, Alba called back, and joyfully reported:

"Vânia, this must be something arranged by God!"

"What happened? Did you get something? Hurry and tell me." Was Vania's anxious response.

"I called Zelia. She said that we could send the father and the daughter to her. They are going to give them all the support they need."

Jumping up and down with the cellular in her hand, Vânia couldn't stop thanking Alba.

"My goodness! How wonderful. What a blessing! You are right, Alba. This must have been arranged by God!"

When Vânia told Zelia the story of that religious man, full of faith, she was surprised by her response:

"Do you know something, Vânia? The Church of Jesus Christ of Latter-day Saints is only a block away from our institution. So, the family will be doubly cared for. Besides, when he gets here to the airport, we are going to take him directly to have a consultation with an ophthalmologist to check his lack of vision."

Vânia was elated with such news. But that was nothing compared with the news that Zelia gave her two weeks after the family had arrived in the small town of Jatai:

"The doctor said Eduardo Villanueva totally lost his vision in his left eye. However, he underwent surgery on his right eye and has recuperated 50% of his vision."

Vânia was overwhelmed and said only:

"Good gracious Zelia! We were looking for a miracle and you were the angel who made this miracle possible."

Often, as I contemplate such episodes, something makes me believe that the hand of God intervenes in favor of those who act to aid their fellow beings and especially, when they act to relieve the suffering of one who seeks relief of the soul. That man, weary of suffering, after losing his wife and son, in spite of his physical deficiency, cared for and supported his only daughter, knowing that she was his greatest treasure. He never lost his faith and, even though only partially, recovered his sight.

The last time I asked our friend Zelia about Eduardo, she told me that he was doing super well. "Don't worry. He works as a gardener for the city. And Carley has gained back her weight. She is already a little chubby."

On the humanitarian mission of assisting refugees, solidarity, compassion and emotion are always in our heart. Every time I think about the following story, I get emotional.

When I first met them, they asked that same question: "Where are we going, Brother Martins?"

"I don't know! You also don't know. Only the Lord knows." I told the family.

"May I ask you a favor?" said the head of the family.

"Yes, of course" was my answer.

"Please send us someplace where there are lots of bees!" was this immigrant's request.

When I first started to write this book, I asked Virginia to tell her own story. I didn't want to miss any detail of her exciting journey leaving Venezuela and coming to Brazil. She recalled that during the first years of her marriage, her husband tried several activities as a breadwinner.

"However, none of his efforts was successful. Discouraged, my husband José, decided to get a steady job, one that would offer us security and stability. He did get a job, and he spent the entire week away from home. He had no time for anything. That is not what we wanted for our family."

After a while, listening to his entrepreneurial spirit, José left the company and decided to work for himself. He would buy fruits in the country and would sell them in the city. As time passed, a recession hit Venezuela's economy.

"Our first child was born. There was no milk in the supermarkets. We had to go out into the countryside searching for cow's milk or goat's milk for the baby. One day, in search for milk, we met a beekeeper who produced honey. My husband was very curious and immediately became interested in learning more about beekeeping and the honey market."

"We prayed to God and José decided to sell honey on the highway that went past the little farm where we lived. We will never forget the date of July 9, 2015. My husband set up a plastic table with 15 jars of honey alongside the highway. He made a sign that read 'Honey for Sale' and waited for clients to come. Soon a car stopped and bought one jar. Then another car stopped and took a jar of honey, then one more. José was super happy with his sales."

For him, who was an optimistic man, the thought was logical:

I have already sold three jars. I still have 12 jars. If things continue like this, by the end of the day, I will have sold them all and I will go home with my pockets full of money.

However, he never could have imagined what was going to happen. All of a sudden, a huge semi-truck went flying by at top speed on the highway. As it passed, the wind was so strong that it picked up the plastic table along with all the jars of honey. The result: 8 jars shattered on the ground. José was able to save only 4 jars. In spite of the accident, José did not give up. He stayed by the highway until he had sold the very last jar.

"When my husband told me the story, I was frantic. I was very sad and mad indeed. But he seemed calm and happy. I wanted to know why and then I asked:

"You just suffered a huge loss on your first day of selling honey and you are still so calm and happy?"

"Yes, my dear." was his answer.

"I can't understand you. Have you suddenly gone mad?" was the wife's reaction.

"Look, sweetheart, I just found out that we have an excellent sales location. Tomorrow will be another day. All we need to do is to arrange a heavier table that will stand up the wind from the trucks."

With that kind of determination, José would wake up early and set up his honey stand at the side of the highway. Each day, sales increased. Until, one day, he returned home with a new idea in his head.

"Sweetheart, we buy honey from the producer. What if we become the producer?" he asked with enthusiasm.

"But what do you know about producing honey?" Virginia asked.

"I don't know anything, but I have been studying and I found out that there are courses that teach how to become a beekeeper."

They soon saved up the money to take the courses and to buy the material to produce their own honey. That is how they bought their first five hives. Then, five more. As time passed, they started to sell honey in large quantities, in various parts of the country. In addition to honey, they sold propolis and royal jelly. Business was growing at an incredible rate. In January, 2018, they were surprised by a burglary. Virginia tells it like this:

"The thieves stole our entire stock of honey. And worst of all, they destroyed our hives. That ruined us financially and emotionally, because we loved our bees and realized their importance to the environment. Due to this incident and since the situation in the country was deteriorating steadily, the decided to pray to God to know what to do".

"The answer was that we should go to Brazil. Although I had faith in that answer, at times I wondered: *What kind of craziness is this? To leave everything behind, our family, our business, everything we had built, our bees!*"

"With hope, courage and faith, we left for Brazil, taking our three children, Anthonella, Simon and José, who got his father's name because he was born on Beekeepers' Day in Venezuela."

"Emotionally, it was a very difficult trip. We cried throughout the whole trip. At that time, my husband was ill. Yet, we knew that we were doing the right thing." She recalls.

They arrived at Boa Vista and we met.

"At that time, we had no idea who Carlos Wizard was. My husband, wanting to impress, told everyone that he was a great entrepreneur in Venezuela."

During my first conversation with José, I asked him:

"In your opinion, what is the greatest business of our time?"

Without hesitation, he answered:

"Petroleum, gold and honey."

I had a good laugh at that unusual answer and then I asked him if he had some preference for any certain city in Brazil.

José quickly answered:

"Please send us to a place where there are many bees."

When I informed them that they would be going to the city of Campos, they asked me:

"Are there lots of bees in Campos?"

I honestly answered them:

"I can't say. I have never been to Campos. I am certain of one thing, though. It does not matter where you go. The Lord will have prepared the way better than you could ever imagine."

I then gave them a book which they consider "one of the best presents they ever received in their life": *Awaken the Millionaire Within.*

Virginia says that for them the book has been fundamental. "It has become a guide for our success in Brazil".

They arrived in Campos on November 20, 2018. José immediately began to look for work. One day, he stopped at a store that specialized in lumber sales:

"I would like to know if you sell wooden beehive boxes." he asked.

To his surprise, the man asked:

"By any chance, are you a beekeeper?"

"Yes," he said. "I have just arrived here from Venezuela and I intend to raise bees in the city."

The man smiled broadly and said:

"Well, then, you are going to help us out. Come with me out to the front of the store. I have something to show you."

Being curious, José accompanied the man to the front of the store, without knowing quite what to expect. Pointing up the top of the storefront, he said:

"Can you see that swarm of bees? It has been there for some time now. We have done everything to get rid of them, but have not been successful. We want to install a lighted billboard there, but no one has the courage to mess with those bees."

At that moment, there occurred one of the many miracles that that family of immigrants enjoyed in Campos. The owner of the store proposed to buy the bee suits, equipment and material needed by a beekeeper, in exchange for José getting the bees away from there.

In the days that followed, José found out that there were other stores in town with the same "problem". He then began to offer his services to those businesses.

One day, I contacted him and asked:

"My friend, José, did you find any bees in Campos?"

To my surprise, he said:

"Yes, yes, Carlos. They are all over the place here. People can't see them, but I see them everywhere I go."

Before they knew it, they had established a small apiary there in Campos and were selling honey to friends, neighbors and stores in town. Soon thereafter, they were interviewed by the local TV station and following that interview, they got calls from several businesses interested in selling their honey.

Virginia continues her story saying: "When we arrived in Boa Vista, we never imagined that we would so quickly get back to raising bees. Our objective now is to increase our business and to have apiaries in different parts of the country. This way, we may become the largest honey producers in Brazil. We will do this by qualifying and training others to understand the potential and importance of bees."

Every day, someone asks José and Virginia:

"Do you ever wish to go back to your country?"

And they respond:

"We miss our country, our family who stayed back there, but Brazil is now our promised land, a land of unequalled opportunities, a country where one can make our dreams come true. We believe that in Brazil we can become prosperous!"

After seeing hundreds of experiences like these, how can one doubt that this is the work of God?

All these stories reveal our insignificance in light of the greatness of our Creator. He could do all this by himself, but he is so merciful that He gives us the privilege of being small instruments in his hands and witnesses of His manifestation in people's lives.

I will close this chapter with an experience that I will never forget. I was preparing to fly to Brasilia. Before leaving, I planned to meet a family that had just arrived from Venezuela. It was almost time for my flight to take off. I had only a few moments available. For an instant, I thought:

Should I go see them or not? Should I talk with the family or not? Will such a short visit make any difference?

On the other hand, I thought:

They have waited for so long for the moment to learn where they will spend, who knows, maybe the rest of their lives.

I followed that inner voice and decided to go quickly to meet them. I arrived where they were, rushing and excusing myself:

"Happy to meet you, I'm sorry, but I only have a few moments. I am on my way to the airport. Can we talk briefly?"

The couple and their children suggested that we sit down and talk a bit. However, I worriedly responded:

"Please forgive me, but, if possible, can we talk standing up? If I stay longer, I run the risk of missing my flight. I have a list of 50 cities offering hosting. In a moment, I will tell you where you will be going."

While I inspected the book with the list of cities, trying to decide where they would go, the father, mother and two children gazed at each other, aware that their destiny, where they would begin a new life in a new country was being decided. Out of all those possible locations, I had a strong feeling about one city.

"You will be going to Curitiba!" I announced.

Then something unexpected happened. The woman hugged me tightly and her tears flowed freely. I was uneasy. I looked at the husband and children but she continued to hug me and to cry. Then I asked:

"Why are you so touched by this announcement?"

"You know, Brother Martins, last night I had a dream. In that dream, I saw our family arriving at the airport in the city of Curitiba."

Then, the one who became emotional was me. We only had time to take a quick photo and I left immediately.

111

During the whole flight I kept thinking about what had just happened. Certain things are beyond our ability to explain. They just happen. They are signs that we are not alone. They are indications that we are being guided by God, who points the way.

When we finally accept that the best is yet to come, we leave everything we desire in God's hands. That is when miracles happen. That is when we flush with emotion for a life we never imagined we could enjoy.

12

THE GOSPEL OF LOVE

As I mentioned before, one of the first people I met in Boa Vista was a businesswoman, Aurea Cruz, who abandoned her businesses in order to feed thousands of people each day at the local Catholic Church. She had come from a traditional family in the city. She was a school teacher, later became the principal of the school, and in her heart, she had the dream of having her own business. Through the years, she saved up enough money to open a pizza place in town.

One day, as she left her home, she was astonished by the number of Venezuelans in the street, in search of food. She then began to carry milk and cookies in her car and whenever she stopped at a stoplight, she would give them out to the refugees.

One day, a priest from the Catholic church called her to say that he was preparing food for the immigrants who were living in the streets and he needed some help. That was back in 2016. At that time, the priest had volunteers who cooked three times a week. They would then go out and distribute the food to the Venezuelans who lived in the streets of Boa Vista.

The women of the church received some donations. Most of the time, however, Aurea would use money from her own pocket to make it possible for the meals to be prepared. At first, they would make 100 meals, then 200 and soon they were preparing 300 meals per day. This happened three times per week. It was something astonishing, because the number of Venezuelans was increasing day by day. They would take the food to those who were begging at stoplights, and that was totally disorganized. People would come running, desperate to get a plate before the food was all gone.

One day Aurea paused to think. She had been born in Boa Vista and loved the city. She did not like going out and seeing so many people begging for money in the streets, as though this were a normal part of the scenery. She began to think:

I need to be proactive. I need to do something to change this reality.

Concerned with this situation, one day she went to the church to talk to the priest:

"You know, Father, no one eats only three times a week, right?"

The priest agreed and from that moment on, they began to prepare food from Monday to Saturday. An ecumenical group of volunteers was formed in which everyone gathered to help. And, as Aurea herself would say, she thus became the city's 'begger'. Wherever she went, she would ask for resources, a sack of rice, beans, potatoes. Before, she thought that she shouldn't announce what she was doing, because one hand shouldn't know what the other is doing. But now, she started to share with everyone what was happening, so that more people could contribute.

She formed a group of volunteers and started to organize those who were willing to donate and those who would do the cooking. She would say: "If you can't bring food for the pot, come and cook the food that's in the pot".

One day, upon arriving at the church, she found out that there was no oil for cooking. "I am concerned about the oil." she said out loud. As if by a miracle, a gentleman arrived with a pick-up truck loaded with bottles of oil and said, jokingly: "Why were you concerned about oil, oh, woman of little faith!"

Fortunately, people of all faiths began to deliver food to the church to help with the meals being distributed by Aurea. She learned then that the miracle of multiplication was possible only through the miracle of sharing. One concept complements the other.

Eight months after she started her work, the first refugee camp was built in the city to remove the 800 people who were living inside the church. On the night that those refugees were removed, seven hundred more who were spread in town showed up in front of the church. It was in a night of heavy rain that Aurea saw the most shocking scene of her life.

"The scene that most affected my life was when 700 people were standing around the Church and I knew that that night we were in for a storm. I also knew that the Army was going to drive refugees out of there and take them to a safe place." These were immigrants who had arrived after the church had been cleared out. They were occupying the streets around the church as a safety zone.

Knowing that the Army bus was going to pick the people up, Aurea was relaxed resting at home. But, suddenly, a torrential rain began to fall on the city and she began to have a strong feeling of concern for the refugees. The rain was as heavy as her apprehension and that caused her to get in her car and speed over to the church. She knew that if the Army had not yet come, she should at least open the front door of the church for the refugees to take shelter inside until the rain let up. When she arrived at the gate of the church, she saw an immense black canvas stretched out on the square. Aurea imagined that everyone had gone to a safe place to be protected against the heavy storm.

They must have left their things under the tarp to protect them from the rain, she thought.

However, when it became obvious that a car had arrived at the church, she saw something she could never imagine. Under that huge tarp there weren't only belongings. There were about 700 people lying on the ground, soaked to the skin. Suddenly, the refugees started coming pouring out from under that tarp. They had not yet been transferred. They were all there, soaking wet, mothers, children in arms and the elderly, wringing wet, trying to escape the torrential rain that showed no sign of diminishing.

For her, the scene was shocking because those people poured out, like ants out of an anthill. "Never in my life did I expect to see such a scene."

She immediately ran to open the door of the church to shelter them until the Army arrived. In that moment, she felt that God had touched her heart to go to rescue and assist vulnerable souls.

What would have happened if Aurea had not appeared? We will never know.

Four years after she created that group of volunteers, the Army installed 12 refugee camps in the city, holding 7 thousand immigrants. Aurea, on her own account, developed a humanitarian action that rely on the support of several religious institutions and on the population of the city in general. Together, they distribute about 50 thousand meals each month.

In this manner, Aurea came to offer meals to the homeless. Religiously, at ten in the morning, all the food was ready to be distributed. "Because hunger does not wait and it is not just because we are doing voluntary work that we can serve every day at a different time." Punctually, at noon, refugees go to an area next to the bus station. The Army organizes the lines where thousands of refugees gather to receive a plate of food.

"The food we take to the bus station is the same food that we eat every day." she admits with the satisfaction of one who knows that you need to serve something that you would like to have in your own home. Aurea continues: "It is not so easy to go to bed each night knowing that the next morning you have the responsibility to feed so many families."

Even today, she suffers when she looks at the poor children begging for food. She often says:

"These poor children had their childhood stolen." she told me with tears in her eyes. "Once at Christmas, we distributed a hotdog and a little toy to each child. One little boy asked me: 'Auntie, can I give back the toy and get two hotdogs instead?'. That broke my heart."

Even with her gratitude for all organizations that support refugees, one day she let her feelings out: "The love that these children need, no agency in the world can supply. People of faith are the first ones to give the affection and love that these little ones need and deserve." She continued: "Sometimes programs promoted by agencies require so many protocols. For hunger and misery, there can be no protocols. Our protocol must be the gospel of love."

It's strange, how you go from being a person who is away from home to a person with no home at all. The place that is supposed to want you has pushed you out. No other place takes you in. You are unwanted, by everyone. You are a refugee.

Clemantine Wamariya

13

WHY HELP FOREIGNERS?

A Bible verse that inspired me every day while working on the refugee cause is this: "Now therefore ye are no more strangers and foreigners, but fellow citizens with the saints, and of the household of God;". (Ephesians 2:19).

This verse makes it very clear that for God, there are no foreigners. We are all His children. Members of his family. He loves all his children unequivocally, regardless of one's nationality or ethnic origin.

Since my arrival in Boa Vista, almost every week I am criticized in social media for my activities to help Venezuelans refugees. People ask me:

"Why are you helping poor people that are foreigners when there are so many poor people in Brazil?"

In the first place, someone who makes such a prejudgment has not taken the trouble to verify what my activities in favor of the needy population in Brazil are. I do not announce it. I do not advertise it, I don't need to advertise it. I am aware of the teaching found in the Sermon on the Mount:

1 Take heed that ye do not your alms before men, to be seen of them: otherwise ye have no reward of your Father which is in heaven.

2 Therefore when thou doest thine alms, do not sound a trumpet before thee, as the hypocrites do in the synagogues and in the streets, that they may have glory of men. Verily I say unto you, They have their reward.

3 But when thou doest alms, let not thy left hand know what thy right hand doeth:

4 That thine alms may be in secret: and thy Father which seeth in secret himself shall reward thee openly.
(Matthew 6:1-4)

I contemplated carefully the verses quoted above before I began writing this book. I never had the intention of this book being considered an act of showing off or of self-promotion. But I also understand that it is of no use to be considered a reference or an inspiration to so many people, as a successful businessman, if those same people did not know what it is that fills my soul.

What fills my soul is not the profit generated by all my companies. What fills my soul is knowing that I am actively engaged in the place where I am needed. This mission keeps me in contact with my purpose in life, which is to love God and serve His children on this earth. At the end, when the story of my life is ultimately told, I hope that someone will say: "There is a man who saw in me more than I could see in myself". And I think this how God looks at us. He sees in us more than we see in ourselves, and with His help, we can become more than we ever thought possible.

Another reason for writing this book is to inspire and invite other business, community leaders and citizens to participate in this goodwill effort. I am fully convinced that when two minds get together committed to achieve a common objective, there comes a third mind that provides solutions to a specific problem. So we do not work alone. The entire result that was reached in this humanitarian effort was possible only through the valuable support of thousands of people all over the country who donated their time and resources to give a hand to refugees who arrived in their city.

Whenever I meet a child, I have the habit of asking his or her age. My wife tells me I need to stop telling those children that they seem bigger and older than they really are. Vânia says this because the Venezuelan children who usually arrive in Boa Vista are below the ideal weight and height. This practice is part of my habit of looking at that little child and imagining how I can instill in him or her the concept that he or she is greater than what the appearance indicates. Besides, I found out every child likes to feel one or 2 years older.

So, anyone who questions the benefit of the assistance given to foreigners doesn't have the slightest idea of the difference between a poor Brazilian and a refugee. A refugee from Venezuela is part of a group of five million people who fled their country because they found themselves in an extreme state of vulnerability, without a minimum of resources to live with dignity.

A refugee is a person who turns on the faucet at home and no water comes out. He tries to turn on a light in his home and there is no electricity. He tries to use the Internet and there is no signal. He sends his children to school and there are no classes. He goes to the market to shop for groceries and there is no food on the shelves. He goes to the pharmacy to buy medication and the shelves are empty. He wants to work but cannot find a job. And if he is lucky enough to have a job, his salary at the end of the month is enough to buy a package of wheat and a half-dozen eggs.

Ask yourself, when did you see a poor person in your country who was faced with this situation? I have never seen anyone.

Another mistake is to think that a refugee is like a beggar, indigent, unqualified, without education or a specific profession. On the contrary, in the case of Venezuelan refugees, the great majority have an academic background and a qualified profession.

Once, while I was driving my car in downtown Boa Vista, I noticed a family sitting under a tree, holding a sign that read: "Looking for work". I stopped the car and went over to meet them. Enmanuel was a metallic construction technician in Venezuela. With his permission, I took a picture of the couple with their six little children and on the same day, I posted them on social media, asking if anyone would like to host the family in some other part of the country.

I received dozens of contacts from companies who were willing to offer a job to him. The family soon left for the south of the country. Presently, Enmanuel works in his profession and supports his family with his own efforts. And all of his children are in school.

On another occasion, I was driving and found a couple at a stoplight. The young man was washing cars' windshields, while his wife was sitting on the sidewalk caring for their two small children. Once again, I stopped the car and went to meet them. To my surprise, he was an agronomy engineer. The wife was also a university student. They left their country, fleeing from hunger. With their permission again, I took a photo of the family and shared their story on social media.

A businessman in the south of Brazil offered the family housing and employment. At this time, Rosmer and his wife Stephanie are both working. This is what motivates us the most about our refugee program. We created a model that fosters self-sufficiency and gives refugees a sense of value and dignity.

Once, I was leaving one of the refugee camps when a lady said:

"Excuse me young man, could you help me?" I was happy she called me as a young man.

"Of course. What do you need?"

"My husband and I need to get away from here. Could you help us?"

"Have you already signed up for the refugees' relocation program?"

"Yes, we have. We are waiting for an answer."

"How long have you been waiting?"

"Seven months."

"Does your process have a problem? Are you lacking some documentation or vaccines? What could be delaying your process?"

"The documentation is all finished and the vaccines as well."

"So, what could be the problem?"

"She answered in a very quiet voice as though she needed to hide something:

"It's because we have many children."

"How many?" I asked.

"We have eight children."

"So, how is that a problem?"

"It is just that priority is given to families who have few children. And they always put us at the end of the line."

As she was talking, it seemed like a movie was playing in my mind. My wife came from a family of eight. I came from a family of seven. That could have been my parents and their children there, waiting in a refugee camp to depart. Perhaps left behind and forgotten because we had a large family.

I then asked to talk to her husband. We went to their tent where I met the husband and their eight beautiful children. All were anxious to leave Boa Vista. As I explained the program to them I said that soon they would leave that awful place. I got emotional when a 5 year old asked me: "Can we leave today?"

They allowed me to take a picture of the family. On the same day I shared their story on social media. I was surprised to see the number of people throughout the country willing to offer a hand to that "huge" family. A few days later the parents and their eight children departed to start a new life. Today, Luis is working, the children are all in school, and looking at the photo of that family in their tent still gives me more motivation to work to see this type of transformation in people's lives.

In terms of territory Brazil is as large as the United States, with a population of over 200 million. The question I ask is how can it be possible that a country of 200 million inhabitants is not able to absorb 15,000 refugees who are still in Boa Vista? Of course, we can. Certainly, a dose of empathy, compassion and solidarity is all we need.

Besides, we are a nation of immigrants. If any Brazilian looks at his family name, he will conclude that his ancestors came from Europe, the Middle East, Africa or Asia. One thing I can guarantee, when the first immigrants came to this continent, they did not come with a suitcase full of money. They may have even come with just the clothes on their backs. But through hard work, they started a new life.

Specialists who study migratory issues in the world affirm that there is no country better prepared to receive immigrants than Brazil. It is interesting to note that at this time more Brazilians have left the country and migrated to Portugal, Spain, Italy, England, the United States, Canada and Australia than the number of immigrants who have arrived in Brazil.

Therefore, the question at the beginning of this chapter, concerning rescuing foreigners, needs to be rewritten. After all, how can we judge who is worthy to receive assistance and who is not? What kind of humanity are we talking about? Should we be charitable only to those we think deserve our aid? In my life, I have sought to follow these verses from the Book of Mormon:

"Think of your brethren like unto yourselves, and be familiar with all and free with your substance, that they may be rich like unto you. But before ye seek for riches, seek ye for the kingdom of God. And after ye have obtained a hope in Christ ye shall obtain riches, if ye seek them; and ye will seek them for the intent to do good—to clothe the naked, and to feed the hungry, and to liberate the captive, and administer relief to the sick and the afflicted.". (Jacob 2:17-19)

We are living on the edge of hell. We have been waiting for so long for the day that the world would hear our voice. I hope it is today.

Zoher, a Palestinian-Syrian Refugee

14

I HAVE AN AUTISTIC CHILD

Each time a family arrived in Boa Vista with an autistic child, my heart would beat a little stronger, my interest increased to know all about the child's history and condition. I would regularly hear the following comments:

"He was born with this illness."

"He is very aggressive."

"He doesn't like to have people around."

"He doesn't like to eat anything."

"He will never be able to do anything on his own."

My son Nicholas is autistic. Somehow, I identified with the challenges, pains and dilemmas of these parents. Although I am not a specialist on autism, I have learned the following:

Autism is not an illness. It is a condition caused by an overall developmental disorder.

Autism has no cure, but can be treated.

Autistic children are not cantankerous. They may have episodes of irritability, of shouting and crying.

Autistic children are not picky eaters. They may be selective about eating. However, they can be stimulated and trained to expand their preferences for a greater number of foods.

Autistic children are not going to learn by themselves to speak as time goes by. They need stimuli to develop communication skills. The earlier stimuli are given, the better will be the results.

Autism does not make a child dependent for the rest of his or her life. It is possible for the child to develop and learn to be an independent and self-sufficient adult, except in rare cases.

Children with autism are not naturally aggressive. On the contrary, they are docile. However, the parents must orient them and train them with utmost patience and love to interact with other children with gentleness and respect.

Autistic children certainly can learn to look others in the eye, hug and kiss their parents and siblings. Once again, this is the parents' mission, and the fruits do not come overnight.

Autistic children can learn to read and write. However, educational flexibility and individualized attention are paramount.

Autistic children should not remain isolated at home, away from society. Limitations in their social graces do not come from their timid nature or because they do not like people. They simply don't know how to relate to others according to conventional patterns.

The autistic are no less intelligent that others. They simply have different ways of interpreting information and of relating to the world.

As I listened to the views of each family with an autistic child, I would relive my own history of success with Nicholas. I would like to share the experiences that I have had with my son.

How did we cope with this condition together?

What were the greatest difficulties?

How were we able to help him understand his condition?

How did we develop his self-esteem?

How did we stimulate his cognitive development?

How did we discover his natural gifts and abilities?

When Nicholas was 3 years old, we lived in a coastal town, near the beach. At night, I would take him, together with his brother, Felipe, for a walk on the beach. Those walks were super pleasant, except when Nicholas kept pushing his one-year-old brother, who would fall down on the sand. It took many walks for Nicholas to stop pushing his little brother. When both of them began going to school, then the pushing was directed toward his classmates. I don't know how many times Vânia was called to the kindergarten because of Nicholas' "aggressiveness".

One characteristic of the autistic is to talk to someone without looking them in the eyes. Vânia would take Nicholas' face in her two hands and look directly in his eyes when she talked to him:

"Nicholas, look in my eyes, son!"

It took a long time before he was able to converse while looking the other person in the eyes.

When Nicholas was 4 years old, at a Church meeting, Vânia had taken sheets of paper and colored pencils to keep Nicholas distracted. When he gave us the drawings, we were astonished. On the sheet of paper, there were more than 10 small dinosaurs, all in movement. All were drawn in three dimensions, running, jumping, fighting. That is when we discovered that this boy had an artistic gift. Over the next few years, with the aid of specialized teachers, he was able to draw more and more elaborate and beautiful drawings.

When he was 10 years old, Nicholas prided himself in saying that he did not learn English from his father. He learned it from video games. Learning a second language was natural for him. He also learned Spanish with ease. Later, when I began learning Mandarin, I decided to test his gift for languages. He took classes from Lisa, our teacher, from Lingbo,

China. He learned the words in Mandarin as easily as he had learned English and Spanish.

Some might say: "So, then, these youngsters with autism are geniuses!!!" In a way, yes! In certain areas of knowledge, they have natural gifts and abilities that are highly developed.

On the other hand, until he was 10 years old, Nicholas had never eaten a banana. He said that it made him feel bad, sick, with nausea. Vânia understood that it was due to his autistic condition. One day, she convinced Nicholas to eat just a small slice of banana. Later on, two slices, then three slices, until he was able to eat a whole banana. Now, the fruit that he eats the most are bananas.

When Nicholas turned 12, I decided to play a trick on him.

"Nicholas, we have a family tradition. When a child turns 12, we go out together to eat pizza."

Up to that point, he had never put a slice of pizza in his mouth. At that time, he had a crush on a girl named Gabrielle. So I decided to use that hook.

"Imagine if Gabrielle found out that you don't eat pizza?"

There was no escape for him. Felipe, Nicholas and I went to the most famous pizza place in town. When the waiter placed a slice of pizza in each plate, Nicholas squirmed in his seat, looked up, then down and pushed the plate away. He wouldn't touch the pizza. Finally, we used the "Vânia" technique.

"Try just a tiny piece, Nick!"

That was all he was able to eat that day. The next week, we returned to the pizzeria for one more little piece and then another and another. What do you think his favorite lunch is today? That's right. Pizza. From Pizza Hut, of course.

These special needs children often exhibit an excessive spontaneity and ingenuity. One time, we were in Hawaii on vacation. Nicholas has had a special interest in super heroes since he was very young. He had several collections of comic books and their characters. His birthday is on the 15th of July. On that very day, there was to be a premiere of a movie about one of his favorite super heroes. Out of the blue, he announced:

Dad, this week, I will be turning 14. Do you know what I want as a birthday present?"

"Tell me, son."

"I want to go to the movie with you and watch the premiere of Spider Man. Do you know what time the film begins?"

"No, I don't know, Nick. Tell me, pal."

"It starts at midnight. Can we go? Can we? Can we go together?"

Well, what will a father not do to please his son? The night of the premiere, Nicholas, Felipe and I arrived at the theater early. We bought popcorn and sat in our assigned seats. When the theater was full and the film was about to start, Felipe and I watched the most unexpected scene of that night. Nicholas got up, walked up in front of the screen, looked at the audience and announced:

"Good evening everyone. Today is my birthday!"

Then, the entire audience began to sing "Happy Birthday" to the boy who spontaneously decided to share that moment with his "friends."

We have a family tradition. Before we go to bed, we have a prayer with our children, we then hug and go to bed. We do this very spontaneously and naturally. Nicholas would pray and then leave the room without hugging anyone. No kissing. No touching.

Several years passed before he would spontaneously give or accept a hug from dad or mom.

You may be wondering why a book about refugees would be citing so many stories about the challenges faced by Nicholas. Touched by all the autistic children I saw in Boa Vista, I decided to create a support group for such families.

My daughter, Priscila, who graduated from Brigham Young University in Laie, Hawaii, has for several years studied the benefits of essential oils to stimulate learning, attention, concentration, memory, reasoning, improved sleep and behavior. With the cooperation of Amanda Vilela, a very well-known occupational therapist in Brasil, specialized in autism, we have voluntarily attended to more than 100 families with autistic children. These parents receive orientation and counseling on how to cope with the day-to-day issues of their children who have this condition.

This book began telling the story of a father and mother who left everything behind in order to give their son the experience of serving a humanitarian mission. Upon arriving in Boa Vista, they were surprised by the news that Nicholas would be subjected to a trial period. Depending on the result of that period, he would either continue on, independent or he would spend the next 2 years with his parents. So, what happened with him? Was he able to overcome? Did he have a relapse? Did he have to stay with his parents? That is what you will find out in the next chapter.

15

WHAT HAPPENS WHEN WIZARD MEETS ULUKAYA?

The title of this chapter could very well be "What Happens When Two Wizards Meet?". Incredibly, both have a very similar life story. They both came from humble families, they were not born in the United States and in their adolescence, they had to work to earn their keep. Carlos sold fruits and vegetables door-to-door. Hamdi worked in the fields in a small village.

Both left their home country to study English in America. Later, they started their own businesses, prospered and became billionaires. Both belonged to a minority group. They are both dedicated to philanthropy, and both have the same passion: helping refugees.

Carlos was born in Brazil and at age 17 arrived in New York with 100 dollars in his pocket. Three days later, he was washing dishes in The Bethwood restaurant in Totowa, N.J. Nine years later, he was accepted to Brigham Young University, where he graduated in Computer Science. Following his graduation in Utah, he returned to Brazil. At age 30, he began teaching English lessons in his home. Later, he opened an

English school called Wizard. That school became the largest chain of language schools in the world with 3,000 units, employing 50 thousand people, and serving millions of students each year in several countries around the world. Later, he sold his company and made it on to the Forbes list of billionaires.

Hamdi Ulukaya was born in a small village in Turkey and at age 22 he arrived in New York to study English. Three years later, he moved to Albany where he studied at the University at Albany. After leaving the university, Ulukaya went to work at a farm in upstate New York. At age 30, Ulukaya opened a small wholesale feta cheese plant of his own. At age 33, Ulukaya decided to buy a fully equipped yogurt factory in South Edmeston, NY, to produce yogurt with a unique recipe. That is how Chobani came to be. The name means "shepherd". The company grew to become the top-selling brand of Greek yogurt in America and operates the largest yogurt facility in the world. Hamdi Ulukaya sold his company and landed on the Forbes list of billionaires.

Someone might ask: What does a book that mainly deals with refugee issues have to do with the story of two business icons?

The answer is that when we are engaged in doing good for our fellow beings, there are no borders. You may be in Turkey, in Brazil or in the United States. Sooner or later, an invisible force will attract people whose hearts are united in the same purpose. And that is what happened when I was at the border between Brazil and Venezuela assisting refugees. One day, I received a message on my cell phone.

"Hi, my name is Yaron Schwartz. I am calling you from New York City. I work for Mr. Hamdi Ulukaya. We have heard about your great work with refugees. Congratulations. Mr. Ulukaya would like to talk to you. Could we set up a call for the two of you to connect?"

Of course, I knew who the famous Mr. Ulukaya was, but why did he want to contact me now? Could this call be a prank or a joke?

Being naturally curious, I arranged for our phone call, which took place two weeks later. To my surprise, on the date and time agreed to, the most polite, kind and enthusiastic person in the world was at the other end of the line. It really was Mr. Hamdi Ulukaya. That was the moment that we discovered how much we had in common. Not only in personal and professional terms, but above all, we discovered that our hearts were devoted to the same passion: identifying, rescuing and caring for refugees around the world.

And so, Hamdi, a shepherd from Turkey, and Carlos, a teacher from Brazil, come together in a cause that is greater than themselves. They are united to help thousands of refugees to regain self-esteem and be able to look for a better life, full of accomplishments, abundance, happiness and peace.

Perhaps the root of this shared concern and desire to work together in such a noble cause is that at one time they, too, found themselves in the shoes of a refugee. At one time, both of them were far from their homeland, far from their families, far from their origin and their culture. They were young and they were alone. They were searching for something. They didn't know exactly what it was. Perhaps they were trying to find themselves. Deep down inside, they were hoping someone would extend a hand to support them in making something of their lives. It is in this spirit and with this resolve that Hamdi and Carlos unite in the worldwide cause at <www.SaveRefugees.net>.

When I began writing this book, I never imagined that one day I would find someone so far away, yet so close to the inclination of my heart. However, this proves that on this planet physical distance is not important. Life will provide the means to unite people who are ready to give of their time, resources, and love for those who are in need. The only distance that exists is the barrier we create when we close our eye to those around us.

The minute that refugees get a job, that's the minute they stop being refugees.

Hamdi Ulukaya

16

WHAT HAPPENED TO NICHOLAS?

Almost 2 years went by since that August 3, 2018 when we arrived in Boa Vista. In spite of all the parents' apprehension, anxiety and worry, not for a single day did Nicholas ever call us asking for any kind of help. There was no emergency situation. No personal or interpersonal crisis. No complication needing major concern.

He spent the first three months near us in Boa Vista. He was then transferred to Parintins, a small town in the middle of the forest, by the margins of the Amazon river, where he served for seven months. Then he was transferred to Vilhena, in Rondônia. Then he came back to Boa Vista for a few months and spent the last six months of his mission in the city of Coari, in the state of Amazonas, where access is only possible by an eight-hour boat ride from Manaus.

During the entire time of his mission, he diligently followed the set program. He contacted thousands of people. He taught hundreds of families the importance of keeping the family united, with Christian principles and values. Every week, he guided people who were interested in knowing more about the Church of Jesus Christ of Latter-day Saints. He baptized dozens of people who accepted the Gospel of Jesus Christ.

During that period, besides other assistance-type activities, he needed to cook his own food, clean his own house, wash his own clothes, and must have walked some three thousand miles, since young missionaries do not have a car and depend on public transportation to get around. That is, he had to act in an independent manner, without any privileges because of his personal, social or financial condition. All he wanted was the opportunity to serve his fellow beings, dedicate himself to a cause, to serve just like 70 thousand other young people who do this voluntary work in many parts of the world.

Should we censure our own desire for our child to feel greater that he or she appears to be? Down deep, we are all greater than we think. But, as others see us as greater than we seem, we begin to understand who we are.

That Carlos, who crossed the border, is no longer the man who left Campinas, headed for Boa Vista. And that Nicholas is also no longer the same. He returns home more mature, more conscientious, and more responsible, with an ample view of the future. Carlos also returns home much expanded, more human, more vulnerable and at the same time stronger.

Our real motive for having gone to Boa Vista was our preoccupation for the well-being of Nicholas. And, as incredible as it may seem, during the time we spent in Roraima, the least of our worries was that of our son. God cared for him so well, so perfectly; much better than we could have done. I am sure that there was not a single day that God ever abandoned him.

I feel that, through my son, the invisible hand of God sent me exactly to the place where I was needed at that moment, sent me the right people, placing them in my path. In the end, he showed me that the fruit of our labors was what happened in the lives of 12 thousand refugees.

I believe that I was able to accomplish much more than I could ever have imagined. My heart is now part of all of Brazil. A heart that has been enriched with so many memories. I continue my life as a dreamer. I believe that we are eternal apprentices. It is clear that at every moment of our lives, we have a different dream. What awaits me after this mission? Perhaps Africa? Perhaps China? Or, who knows, Brasília? I'll go where you want me to go, dear Lord!

As you read this book, it is my hope that you will find a mission that will cause changes in your life and in the lives of people around you, that it may touch your heart and push you to dream in search of your true purpose in existing.

As I close this book, I hope that you will find in your soul, the answer that you so anxiously seek: a life's project capable of transforming your destiny and taking you on unimaginable flights. A way of generously contributing to the world. These are the words of someone who knows what money can bring, and who has had the satisfaction of fulfilling a mission that could never be bought with money.

Participating in this humanitarian action was one of my greatest undertakings, one of the greatest voyages I have ever taken. It was a path that helped me to forget myself, my comfort and my convenience and to give of myself totally to my fellow beings. It forced me to make a new pact with life. We left home without knowing what was in store for us, but we return home with the feeling of having fulfilled a mission of love, a mission of faith, a mission of life.

I'm the daughter of refugees.
The immigrant mentality is to
work hard, be brave, and never
give up in your pursuit of
achieving the American dream.

Reshma Saujani

EPILOGUE

It was March of 2020. Vânia and I left Boa Vista with a heavy heart. We still had four more months to complete our refugee service assignment. However, an invisible enemy, the most feared on the planet, finally made its appearance in the rain forest. The arrival of COVID-19 had been the thing that was most feared by the local population. This devastating enemy had already spread through Asia, Africa and North America. Now it had arrived in the Amazon. All the countries in South America closed their borders. No more refugees from Venezuela could come into Brazil.

The people in the little city of Boa Vista were in despair. Vânia and I as well. We were told that we were immediately to return home to Campinas. We left without taking anything. We abandoned our cars, furniture, household items and clothing. But those things had no value to us, anyway. What Vânia and I most regretted was leaving behind those 15,000 refugees, without knowing what their destiny would be. How could they practice social distancing when the most common living arrangement in the city was to have twenty people piled up in the same little house? In the refugee camps set up by the UN, the standard was to have two families, each with three or four small children, occupying the same tent. How could they avoid physical contact among such little ones? It would be impossible.

I returned home to Campinas, but my heart remained behind in Boa Vista with the refugees.

I was safe in quarantine in my home, but what about those 15,000 refugees left behind? I desired to share with the whole world my experiences, emotions, and lessons learned during my twenty months living with the refugees and the urgent need to continue to help these vulnerable families.

From the moment I got home, my mind kept thinking on how to rescue those refugees that stayed behind. I wanted to get this message out right away in the hopes to find a solution. During those days I felt uncomfortable, uneasy, anxious. How could those refugees be saved as soon as possible?

Then, late one night, unable to sleep, the inspiration came: *Carlos, the book about refugees is ready to go out to the world. You are going to launch this book immediately. This is the time when people most need a message of faith, hope, and love! Through this book, you will raise a greater humanitarian cause, to instill love in the hearts of people, and to support those refugees that stayed behind in the Amazon.*

That is how this book you are now reading came about. The story contained in this book, and the case it supports, is so noble that it cannot have commercial purpose. It can only be acquired through the generous donations of its readers in promoting an even greater good. 100 percent of proceeds of this book will be fully used to assist refugees who are stranded in Boa Vista and need to start a new life in other parts of the country. I believe that both you and I are now in quarantine, perhaps distressed with being confined at home, wondering about the future and whether life will ever return to normal. In many ways, this is what a refugee's life is like. I lived for almost 2 years with people who had absolutely nothing, who wondered whether they would ever find a new beginning where they could live in peace and security, and provide for their families. As they sit confined in tents, with limited means to provide for themselves, to use their skills, or to educate their children, they also wonder about the future and whether their lives will ever return to normal. Or will they be stuck, waiting, forever?

Through your generosity, together we can make a difference in the lives of thousands of refugees now. Because I believe that even if the virus stays with us for months, we will all be able to rise up again, rebuild our lives from where we left off, and in addition, look around to find others who might need our support. We will thus be united in a great humanitarian cause; whether it be to rescue refugees suffering from the economic crisis or give relief to those infected with a virus.

Whatever cause is within your reach, embrace it with faith, and without fear. If you do so, you will be filled with the unfailing love of God. You will become a source of blessings to all those around you, wherever you go and you will become an instrument in the hands of God to bless his children here on earth.

Believe me. The fact that you have acquired this book and have felt the importance of its message means that a good seed has been planted in your heart. That seed will surely bring forth good fruit in your life. And you can be the means of planting many more good seeds in the lives of refugees. Seeds of hope in the good news of a new life that is yet to come.

**Refugees are going to continue
to come, and the only question
is what we are going to do to
help them.**

Davan Yahya Khalil

Release in association with Refúgio 343, which will benefit from
part of the sales revenue of the book."

FONTS Greta Text, Druk, Replica

Made in United States
Orlando, FL
16 January 2024

42559721R00088